HEALTH CARE REFORM SIMPLIFIED

WHAT PROFESSIONALS IN MEDICINE, GOVERNMENT, INSURANCE, AND BUSINESS NEED TO KNOW

Dave Parks

Health Care Reform Simplified

Copyright © 2012 by Dave Parks

ISBN-13 (pbk): 978-1-4302-4896-5
ISBN-13 (electronic): 978-1-4302-4898-2

President and Publisher: Paul Manning
Lead Editor: Jeff Olson
Technical Reviewer: Beth Brophy
Editorial Board: Steve Anglin, Mark Beckner, Ewan Buckingham, Gary Cornell, Louise Corrigan, Morgan Ertel, Jonathan Gennick, Jonathan Hassell, Robert Hutchinson, Michelle Lowman, James Markham, Matthew Moodie, Jeff Olson, Jeffrey Pepper, Douglas Pundick, Ben Renow-Clarke, Dominic Shakeshaft, Gwenan Spearing, Matt Wade, Tom Welsh
Coordinating Editor: Rita Fernando
Copy Editor: Kimberly Burton-Weisman
Compositor: Bytheway Publishing Services
Indexer: SPI Global
Cover Designer: Anna Ishschenko

Distributed to the book trade worldwide by Springer-Verlag New York, Inc., 233 Spring Street, 6th Floor, New York, NY 10013. Phone 1-800-SPRINGER, fax 201-348-4505, e-mail orders-ny@springer-sbm.com, or visit http://www.springeronline.com.

For information on translations, please contact us by e-mail at **rights@apress.com**, or visit www.apress.com.

Apress and friends of ED books may be purchased in bulk for academic, corporate, or promotional use. eBook versions and licenses are also available for most titles. For more information, reference our Special Bulk Sales–eBook Licensing web page at www.apress.com/bulk-sales.

*To the health care providers who are still able
to put their passion in compassion*

Contents

About the Author

Dave Parks has more than 25 years of experience as a journalist, and he has earned numerous awards for his coverage of some of the most important medical issues of our time. His investigative reporting about health problems found, but ignored, in veterans of the 1991 Persian Gulf War led to a White House investigation, Congressional hearings, and changes in how the military screens troops medically before and after battle. He has written in-depth, groundbreaking stories about cancer survivorship, health disparities, cervical cancer prevention, and liver transplantation. He has worked as an editor and writer in the Midwest and the Southeast, and he has traveled to some of the deepest reaches of Africa to cover the AIDS pandemic. He is a member of the Association of Health Care Journalists and the American Medical Writers Association.

About the Technical Reviewer

Beth Brophy is a writer and editor who writes frequently about health issues. She is an associate editor and the podcast producer for *Health Affairs*, a leading health policy journal. She has been a senior editor at *US News and World Report*, a columnist for *USA Today*, and a reporter at *Forbes* magazine. She is the author of two non-fiction books and a novel. She lives in Chevy Chase, MD. Her BA is from William Smith College, and she has a master's degree in journalism from Northwestern University.

Acknowledgments

I'm always a little sheepish about putting my name on any collaborative work of journalism, which in my mind includes nearly all writing found in books, magazines, and newspapers. It may be necessary to name the author of a work, but a single byline takes for granted a complex editorial process. For a writer, the road to publication is filled with editors who vet, correct, and polish the work, not to mention graphic artists and skilled workers who are also in the production cycle. At least four editors gave constructive criticism, checked facts, copyedited, and supplied technical support for this book. Along with improvements, they also provided words of encouragement. I thank them.

This book also was made possible by a host of sources—print journalists, bloggers, medical authorities, and policy experts who produced a mountain of articles and papers about day-to-day developments and trends surrounding health care reform. I've listed many of them in the bibliography, but it would be difficult to name everything I've read on such a pivotal issue. Please forgive any omission.

As with any book like this, a writer must depend upon some trusted sources. Fortunately for me, the Henry J. Kaiser Foundation, The Commonwealth Fund, and the Robert Wood Johnson Foundation provided Internet portals leading to a massive body of studies, articles, graphs, charts, and papers on health care reform. In many ways, foundations provided the foundation for this book. Understand though, that these private foundations do approach the subject of health care reform with a point of view toward promoting a medical system that provides the best service to the most people at the most efficient cost. To many people those would be laudable goals, but health care reform is a contentious issue with many diverse points of view. Still, these foundations are generally non-partisan, and it's difficult to dispute most of the facts they provide.

Finally, I must acknowledge my family's impact on my own point of view in writing this book. In recent years, I watched as my mother and father aged, grew frail, and came to depend upon American medicine. I saw the best and the worst of the system. My parents are both gone now, leaving behind a final, influential lesson in courage, compassion, and care. I must thank my wife, Barbara, a registered nurse, for her patience, support, and wisdom. Additionally, I tested many of my writing approaches on my son, Mitchell; daughter, Laura; and son-in-law, Nick Wong. They may not have known it, but their responses helped shape my attempts to explain a complicated subject.

Introduction

It's November 2004, and I'm in an operating room at the University of Alabama at Birmingham Hospital watching a 57-year-old Alabama schoolteacher slipping into the emptiness of anesthesia. She's grasping a vision of life, of a grandson nestled in her arms. "I'm holding my baby here," she says, her voice relaxed and peaceful amid choreographed movements of doctors, nurses, and medical technicians. An anesthesiologist places a mask over her face. She inhales and fades away.

More than six hours later, she awakens in an intensive-care bed and has a transplanted liver, along with the opportunity to again hold grandchildren close and feel love, hope, and humanity. She is among more than 65,000 Americans who have undergone this dramatic operation since 1988. The cost: roughly a quarter million dollars each.

A few months later, I'm standing in tropical humidity, among single-story, whitewashed buildings comprising Lewanika General Hospital in Western Zambia. I'm in an outdoor waiting area that is packed with members of the Lozi Tribe, people who still live in picturesque villages of grass huts in sub-Saharan Africa. There are few chairs, and people mostly stand or sit on cement sidewalks. Chickens living on the hospital grounds occasionally squawk their way through the crowd. Two women wail pitifully, having just received word of a death.

About a dozen mothers sit on gurneys and nurse newborns in a ward that is nothing more than a long, open room. Two nurses in starched, white uniforms walk the hallway wearily. They work thirteen-hour shifts, four days a week, and earn the equivalent of $25 a week. The hospital lacks oxygen equipment, thermometers, blood pressure machines, and basic pharmaceuticals such as antibiotics. Patients are asked to bring their own drugs if they can afford them. Equipment in surgical suites is old and worn, with rubber cracked and crumbling.

The United States has one of the richest health care systems in the world, and Zambia one of the poorest. Zambia spends about $80 a year per person on health care; the United States spends about $8,000. Both countries struggle to provide enough good quality health care for everybody.

Zambia has been reforming its health care system since 1992. It's been tough. About one in seven of Zambia's adults live with HIV/AIDS. There's no insurance to speak of, and if policymakers raise the price of care, nobody can afford it; if they drop the price to nothing, patients swamp the system. There's only so much to go around, and in an impoverished nation, few people can afford to pay much of anything, particularly in rural areas.

America is reforming its health care system, too, with the Patient Protection and Affordable Care Act of 2010. The United States has the most expensive health care on earth, but the quality and quantity can be spotty. Extraordinary medicine, probably the best in the world, is practiced at places like the Cleveland Clinic, Mayo Clinic, and the Johns Hopkins Medical Center, but many publicly supported hospitals for indigent care can be pretty spartan. Go to impoverished rural areas of a state like Alabama, and medicine gets even more basic—and scarce. Medical errors are a problem everywhere.

Be assured, though, from the bush of Zambia to a modern operating room of an American medical center, there is a fundamental drive among people to provide each other with decent health care. It's a basic human value. Who pays is another matter entirely, particularly in America.

For example, a 2009 CBS News poll found that 64 percent of Americans believe the government should guarantee health insurance for everybody. Fine, but a Penn Schoen Berland poll the same year asked people if they were willing to pay more taxes to guarantee this health coverage, and the same exact same portion of Americans, 64 percent, said no.

Still, if somebody shows up at a hospital emergency department in the United States with a medical need and he can't afford to pay, he must be seen. A sense of common decency among Americans led to a law, enacted 25 years ago, requiring hospitals to accept these types of patients. Most people didn't realize it at the time, but that was a turning point in American medicine, when the nation decided that everybody deserved some level of care.

It is called the Federal Emergency Treatment and Labor Act of 1986. It requires hospital emergency departments to provide examination and, if needed, emergency care, regardless of ability to pay. The care, which is usually uncompensated, doesn't end at the emergency department. If a woman comes in about to have a baby, she stays at the hospital until the baby is delivered. If a man comes in riddled with gunshot wounds, he goes to surgery and stays in the hospital until he can be safely discharged.

The US Supreme Court has ruled on the law, and left it intact. But the law is criticized because at times it appears to open the US health care system to exploitation. Studies show that up to 55 percent of an emergency physician's time may be spent delivering this care after doing tests to determine if these patients have an "emergency medical condition"—a term that has a fuzzy legal definition. This contributes significantly to emergency department over-crowding, and the law does not provide a way to pay for exams and care. We all foot the bill in one way or another. And to make things worse, this type of crisis care is extremely expensive and often would be unnecessary if the patient had decent medical care to begin with.

Still, the law stands, and the current debate is not over whether we should provide care to everybody. It is about where the care is going to be delivered, how good the care is going be, and how we are going to pay for the care. It's also about what we are going to do about more than 50 million Americans who lack insurance.

We're trying to find a way to make our health care system work in a humane way for patients, an affordable way for consumers, and a profitable way for insurers and providers. We want all this, and we also want to keep the miracles of modern American medicine. We want high-ticket procedures like $750,000 heart transplants, $325,000 open-heart surgeries, and $150,000 eye operations. We want more preventive care for everybody. We want fewer medical errors, and more evidence-based treatments. And we want lower medical costs and insurance premiums, with taxes for health care kept to a minimum.

That's a pretty tall order for a complex, $2.3 trillion-a-year medical system.

Already, two years into health reform, we're seeing how complicated the process can be. Under the new health laws, insurance exchanges were temporarily established in 2010 for uninsured people with pre-existing medical conditions. The US Department of Health and Human Services (HHS) predicted that 375,000 people would be enrolled at these exchanges by the end of 2010. By February 2012, the enrollment stood at about 50,000.

It's a living demonstration that better and more available insurance doesn't always translate into fewer uninsured people. Cost is always an issue, but so too are culture, faith, education, awareness, and trust.

For example, when American doctors first arrived in Zambia to help with the AIDS pandemic, they established a clinic in Lusaka, a city with a population of over 3 million, and starting taking blood samples from Zambians to see if they were HIV positive. Soon, people stopped coming to the clinic. When doctors asked why, Zambians said word had gotten out that their blood was being used in demonic rituals.

That's less preposterous than it sounds. In this country, some people belong to religions that view medical care as a sin. Other people just plain mistrust modern medicine, and wouldn't go to a doctor if you paid them. Others may be unaware of choices—the main problem with low enrollment at the new insurance exchanges for people with pre-existing conditions, federal officials say.

This goal of this book is to raise awareness about what the Patient Protection and Affordable Care Act of 2010 offers different people in different circumstances in as simple a way as possible. It explains how the new health law came into existence, what it provides, and its possible future. The book does not intend to judge whether the new law is good, bad, or ugly. It's about what the law means to individuals, families, businesses, and Medicare and Medicaid recipients. It also explains the impact of the law on insurers, hospitals, and doctors—and how that may affect patients.

It will provide information on new health insurance exchanges, mandates for individuals to have insurance, penalties for failure to have insurance, options for businesses to cover their employees, and much more.

Some things have changed since the first edition of this book was published in 2011. Most notable was a Supreme Court ruling that upheld major provisions of health care reform but complicated efforts to expand the nation's Medicaid program. In addition, the HHS has issued a multitude of rules and regulations affecting many key provisions of health care reform. This second edition will include critical updates and again attempt to gauge the future direction of health care reform.

A few words of caution: Writing about the direction of health care reform is like trying to hit an erratically moving target. For example, when I wrote the first edition of this book, many experts agreed that the future of health care reform would be determined by the Supreme Court ruling. Well, the Supreme Court ruled, and now many experts agree that the future of health care reform will be determined by the outcome of the 2012 presidential election. After that, I'm sure there will be another critical event shaping the future of health care reform. Clearly, massive changes unleashed by the Patient Protection and Affordable Care Act of 2010 remain politically potent, and likely will stay at the forefront of public debate for many years.

Overview

Health Care Reform Past and Future

Americans have been reforming their health care system for more than 75 years, experimenting with treatments, payment methods, and administration. Some of these experiments have worked; others have failed.

The new Patient Protection and Affordable Care Act, signed March 23, 2010, by President Barack Obama, is just the latest and one of the most ambitious attempts to reshuffle America's health care system.

Each generation makes additions, subtractions, divisions, and multiplications to elements of the system, based largely upon expectations, needs, and values. In many ways, American health care is more of a process than a system.

Look back over recent years, and you'll see an alphabet soup of popular innovations like health maintenance organizations (HMOs); preferred provider organizations (PPOs); and point of service plans (POS). Still more confusing, these cost-saving measures were all MCOs, or managed care organizations. That doesn't even include the public side of recent insurance changes, including the Children's Health Insurance Program, also known as CHIP.

Now look into the near future, and at least the acronyms diminish. But the new health care law brings with it its own lingo, including terms like insurance exchanges, individual mandates, grandfathered health plans, health tax credits, guaranteed availability of insurance, and essential health benefits. Alphabet lovers need not to worry, though, since we are getting ACOs, or accountable care organizations.

Understanding the intricacies of all this is fairly daunting—and probably unnecessary for many people. America is a nation in which many people would rather do their own plumbing than do their own taxes. Only the few, the brave, and the wonks will learn all complexities of the new health care law so that they can make an informed purchase of medical insurance.

On the other hand, it is essential to know the basics of the new law, especially if you work in a medical field, many areas of government, or have a business in which you must make informed decisions about how to best provide coverage to your employees. This book strives to plow through bureaucratic blabber and political posturing, and translate provisions of the new health care law into understandable terms. Jump around the chapters and subheads. There won't be a test, other than figuring out how the law best applies to what you do.

This first chapter provides a quick historical perspective on American health insurance and takes a brief look at the political process that brought us health care reform. Then the chapter moves on to a summary of the law, and ends with a timeline for implementing major provisions.

Quick History of Health Care Insurance

American leaders as far back as President Theodore Roosevelt in 1912 have tried to create insurance plans that guaranteed medical coverage for Americans. Success has usually come in relatively small increments, with a few notable exceptions like Medicare and now the new health care law. There has always been strong opposition to this trend toward socialized or nationalized medicine. These two opposing forces have created a hybrid—a public and private partnership that now insures about 85 percent of Americans.

The American health insurance movement first gained traction and speed around the time of World War II with the advent of medical breakthroughs such as the use of plasma to treat shock, surgical techniques to repair defects of the heart and other organs, and the discovery of antibiotics and other drugs to cure once-deadly illnesses.

People wanted these treatments and needed a way to pay for them. They turned to public and private health insurance.

World War II Spurs Insurance Growth

The Second World War provided fertile ground for the rise of insurance. Just before the war, in 1939, only about 10 percent of Americans had private health insurance, and there was little federal involvement with public health care.

Blue Cross insurance plans covering hospitalizations and Blue Shield insurance plans covering doctor visits started just before the war. During the conflict, employers used the plans as a way to attract and keep workers at a time of wage and price controls.

INSURANCE: A MODEL AS OLD AS HAMMURABI'S CODE

Policies offered by private insurers are based upon a common model for a social contract that spreads risks—so that no one person gets overwhelmed by a catastrophic loss.

Insurance has been around a long time; the ancient Hammurabi's Code includes a basic insurance policy.

It typically works like this: premiums from policyholders are pooled, and when somebody needs medical care, costs are paid from the pool. However, the sickest members get the most benefits, and the healthiest members get the least.

It's a simple formula, but it requires highly trained statisticians, or actuaries, to work out the details. And insurers can adjust the formula for competitive purposes by restricting coverage for sickest clients and thus keep their policies more affordable for healthy clients.

Thus, between 1940 and 1945, the types of Blue Cross plans grew from 56 to 80, and enrollment jumped from 6 million to 19 million Americans. Blue Shield had about 3 million members at war's end.

Meanwhile, the government was faced with the responsibility of caring for 15 million returning military veterans, including 671,817 who had been wounded, and hundreds of thousands of dependents left in need.

General Omar N. Bradley oversaw expansion of a government-run health care system under the Bureau of Veterans Affairs. The system now operates under the US Department of Veterans Affairs (VA) and has a $50 billion annual health budget.

Nonprofit Blue Cross and Blue Shield plans began close cooperation in postwar America. They would eventually merge, but in the 1950s, they were separate and began to face competition from a rising number of commercial insurance companies.

THE VA: AMERICA'S NATIONALIZED HEALTH CARE

Most people don't think of it that way, but the US Department of Veterans Affairs is America's system of fully nationalized health care. Of the nation's 23 million veterans, 8.3 million—about the population of Virginia—receive VA care.

The VA foots the bill, although it gets some reimbursement from private and public insurers, and it also manages more than 200,000 administrators, doctors, nurses, and other health professionals. It operates 152 hospitals and 784 outpatient clinics.

In 2010, the VA reported that its facilities handled 75.6 million outpatient visits, an increase of about one-third since 2003. Its inpatient admissions in 2010 totaled 679,600. The VA charges some co-pays, but those are relatively low and don't apply to all veterans.

Over the years, there have been highly publicized complaints about VA care, but studies have given good marks to the overall health care and patient satisfaction.

Health care reform is not expected to have an impact on the VA system. However, the health care law does say VA medical care meets standards for fulfilling the individual mandate for Americans to have medical coverage by 2014. Therefore, veterans receiving VA care don't have to buy more coverage, although they can.

By the mid 1950s, about two-thirds of Americans were insured by private for-profit and nonprofit companies. People got policies through work, but private insurers were reluctant to provide affordable policies to people outside the workforce who incurred high medical costs, including the elderly and disabled.

In 1945, President Harry S. Truman whetted the public appetite for a government solution. He attempted to enact a compulsory health insurance plan for the nation. It failed in Congress, and he then developed a plan to provide free hospital care for Social Security recipients. The American Medical Association and many Republican politicians vehemently opposed the idea of government involvement in health care. They feared a government takeover of health care would strip physicians of autonomy.

In an attempt to find a state-based solution, President Dwight Eisenhower in 1960 signed the Kerr-Mills Act. It provided states with federal grants that could be used to pay medical bills for the indigent and elderly. Only 28 states decided to participate, and many kept budgets for the program too low to meet needs.

President John F. Kennedy supported a move to Medicare during his run for office in 1962, and even his opponent, Richard M. Nixon, agreed that Kerr-Mills was too little, too late. At the time, there were about 20 million Americans over age 65, and even though more than 700 private insurance companies were selling policies, only half the elderly could afford them. Still, Kennedy failed to convince Congress to approve a Medicare program.

Assassination Turns Nation to Medicare

Two things occurred that changed health history: President Kennedy was assassinated in 1963, creating a swell of emotional support for the issues he championed; and his successor, President Lyndon Johnson, won the 1964 election by a landslide that included Democratic majorities in the House and Senate.

Riding this wave of support, Johnson signed Medicare into law on July 20, 1965, with Truman standing by and enrolling as the first beneficiary. That same day, Johnson also signed into law the federal Medicaid program, which provides medical benefits to the impoverished.

Many doctors were incensed, calling the government action the beginning of socialized medicine. Other opponents predicted the nation was on the road to rationed care, and patients would lose the right to choose their own doctor.

Nonetheless, the Blue Cross and Blue Shield plans were among the first to benefit from Medicare and Medicaid. The federal government hired the Blues to oversee Medicare, and many states (which are responsible for administering Medicaid) also turned to the Blues for administrative assistance.

America's Breathtaking Rise of Medical Care Costs

Both private and public insurers quickly began struggling with rising health care costs, which tripled between 1967 and 1981 and then kept rising. A host of medical trends drove the increases, and included more doctors becoming specialists, hospital care getting more expensive, inflation running rampant, and research creating new medical technology and better drugs. Health care costs have increased and are high in other countries, too, but the United States leads the world in the amount spent for medical care, as shown in Figure 1-1.

Insurers tried a number of cost-cutting measures, including the creation of health maintenance organizations, shorter hospital stays, more outpatient surgery, and more preventive care practices. In the early 1980s, the government introduced a new reimbursement system, diagnostic-related groups (DRGs), in an effort to contain Medicare costs.

Amid the rising costs, there were efforts to get more Americans more medical care. In 1986, Congress passed the Consolidated Omnibus Budget Reconciliation Act, or COBRA, which allows workers to continue medical coverage for 18 months after leaving a job; but it was an expensive fix for a worker who had to make up for subsidies that had been paid by a former employer. Also under COBRA were laws requiring hospitals to treat patients regardless of the ability to pay.

In 1988, President Ronald Reagan signed the Medicare Catastrophic Coverage Act, which set ceilings on payments to hospitals, doctors, and prescription

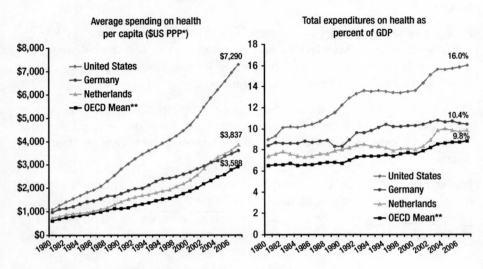

International Comparison of Spending on Health, 1980–2007

Figure 1-1. Comparison of health care costs internationally. The United States leads the world. Source: Commonwealth Fund.

drugs, and included a premium raise and surtax on some Medicare recipients. After a public outcry, the law was repealed in 1989—an indication that sometimes what is done by Congress can be quickly undone.

During the 1990s, health care costs escalated again, rising at twice the rate of inflation. In 1993, President Bill Clinton attempted to reform health care by providing universal coverage and "managed competition" among insurers. The effort, headed by the president's wife, Hillary, failed because of its complexity and strong opposition from the health care industry.

In 1997, Clinton signed legislation to create the Children's Health Insurance Program, an extension of Medicaid that now covers more than 7 million children.

Political Primer on Health Care Reform

As the 2008 presidential campaign approached, the overall cost of American medical care had increased 1600 percent since 1970, nearly three times the rate of inflation. The nation was spending about $2.2 trillion a year on health care, a figure that was projected to double by 2018.

Americans felt the financial burden. Private medical insurance premiums had more than doubled over the previous decade while insurers raised co-pays and deductibles. The percentage of uninsured adults had been creeping up for years and hovered around 15 percent. That meant 46.5 million Americans were uninsured in 2006, leaving one in every six adults under age 65 without medical coverage.

An October 2007 Kaiser Commission study on Medicaid and the uninsured, titled "The Uninsured, A Primer," showed that most uninsured people came from working families. They had jobs where health benefits were not offered by employers, or they were not eligible for coverage under a spouse's plan. About half of undocumented immigrants lacked health insurance, but 78 percent of all uninsured adults in the United States were either native or naturalized American citizens.

Whenever the economy suffered, the ranks of the uninsured swelled as struggling businesses were forced to lay off workers or pull coverage from employees. Meanwhile, insurance premiums kept rising, as illustrated in Figure1-2.

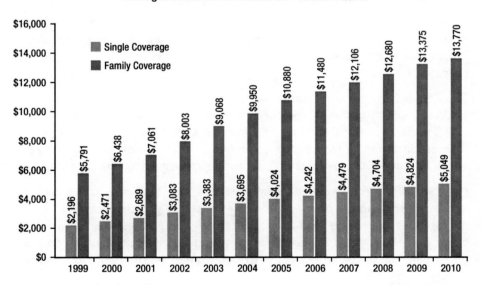

Average Annual Health Insurance Premium Costs

Source: "Employer Health Benefits 2010 Annual Survey," (#8085) The Henry J. Kaiser Family Foundation and HRET, September 2010

Figure 1-2. The steady and dramatic rise of life insurance rates, which more than doubled in a decade. Source: This information was reprinted with permission from the Henry J. Kaiser Family Foundation.

Research showed that uninsured Americans were more sick, less likely to have a regular doctor, less likely to have preventive care, and more likely to be hospitalized for avoidable medical problems. Uninsured people paid only about a third of their medical bills, often with out-of-pocket cash, before receiving services.

Meanwhile, the ranks of Medicare beneficiaries had grown to about 45 million by 2007, and accounted for about a fifth of all national health spending. The baby boomers were headed in the program's direction, and projections indicated that spending would greatly outstrip revenues if something wasn't done.

Making matters worse, globalization was pitting American and foreign labor against each other, and the high cost of insuring US workers was hampering the nation's ability to compete internationally. As the price of insurance rose, fewer employers were offering it as a benefit, and workers were being asked to pay a larger portion of premium costs.

Health Care Enters the 2008 Presidential Campaign

Given developments, the issue of health care was certain to surface in the presidential campaign, and candidates from both major parties presented health care reform plans, though they were very different in philosophy and scope.

The Republican nominee, Senator John McCain, predicted that the health care system would "implode" if something wasn't done about rising costs, and his plan focused on ways to stem the increases. McCain wanted to create a national insurance marketplace to increase competition among insurers, which he said would lower premiums and increase choices for consumers.

He also favored changing the way Medicare and Medicaid paid providers, improving the quality of care and allowing states greater leeway in determining how to provide care for patients with the greatest needs. He advocated giving Americans tax-sheltered health savings accounts, a tax credit for purchasing health insurance, and better consumer information about medical quality.

The Democratic nominee, Senator Barack Obama, had developed a plan that was more complex and more directly addressed the issue of uninsured Americans. Among other things, Obama advocated strengthening employer-based coverage, making insurance companies more accountable, improving quality of care, and ensuring a patient's ability to choose a doctor without government interference. He would allow people to keep their existing health plans, and he promised an initial drop in costs of $2,500 for them.

For people without health insurance, Obama guaranteed them eligibility for insurance. He promised individuals, families, and small businesses new exchanges that would pool customers and keep premiums affordable. He promised to do more about preventing fraud and waste in Medicare and Medicaid. He said that he opposed mandating that all Americans purchase insurance, but did favor penalizing employers who did not provide insurance for workers.

Obama won the election with 53 percent of the vote, and carried Democratic majorities into the House and Senate.

SPEECHWRITER'S "WHIM" SPARKS HEALTH REFORM

Sometimes big political issues have little starts, and health care reform was sort of like that in the 2008 presidential campaign.

According to *Revival: The Struggle for Survival Inside the Obama White House* by Richard Wolffe (Crown, 2010), several of the people on Barack Obama's speechwriting team were under pressure to decide what the president-to-be should say during a speech to Families USA, a patient-advocacy organization. The campaign lacked a health policy, and staffers hadn't spent much time even discussing it.

On a "whim," according to a staffer who was there, Robert Gibbs suggested that Obama promise to enact universal health care for Americans within a year of taking office. The idea stuck. And when Obama spoke the words, members of Families USA went off like a "bomb" the staffer recalled.

That was the seed of the health care reform idea. The plan evolved into a complex campaign promise, and became the first major initiative of the Obama Administration.

Washington Battles over Health Care Reform

Books have been written about President Obama's triumph in pushing health care reform through Congress amid Democratic infighting and Republican opposition. It would be impossible to do the story justice in a few paragraphs, but the highlights are worth mentioning.

Early in his push for health reform, President Obama said he realized that an individual mandate requiring virtually every American to buy insurance was unavoidable. If the government was going to force insurance companies to sell policies to people with pre-existing medical conditions, then the pool of policyholders had to be large enough to cover higher treatment costs for insurers, he said.

Obama was committed to health care reform both politically and personally. His staff connected him with people who would be helped by insurance reform. They included Natoma Canfield, a 50-year-old cancer survivor who was paying $6,000 a year for health coverage she received through an employee-sponsored plan that matched her payment with $1,000. She had been notified that her rate was going up 40 percent the next year. Obama occasionally read her letter before going into meetings to hammer out details about health care reform, according to Wolffe's *Revival: The Struggle for Survival Inside the Obama White House.*

Obama Targets Insurers Despite Their Support

In fact, stories like Ms. Canfield's may have been why Obama shifted his political tactics, and instead of targeting Republican opponents, he focused on insurance companies. Many of these insurers actually supported Obama's health care reform plan, but they also came to symbolize the need for reform.

At one point, when Obama's push for reform was waning, Anthem Blue Cross of California sent letters to customers saying it was raising rates by 40 percent. News coverage of the story breathed new life into Obama and proponents of health care reform.

Shortly afterward, on March 3, 2010, Obama spoke to a small group of doctors and nurses about health care reform, casting himself as a centrist, and saying:

> On one end of the spectrum, there are those who have suggested scrapping our system of private insurance and replacing it with a government-run health care system. And though many other countries have such a system, in America it would be neither practical nor realistic. On the other end of the spectrum, there are those, and this includes most Republicans in Congress, who believe the answer is to loosen regulations on the insurance industry—whether it's state consumer protections or minimum standards for the kind of insurance they sell. ... I disagree with that approach. I'm concerned that this would give the insurance industry even freer rein to raise premiums and deny care. ... The proposal I put forward gives Americans more control over the health insurance and their health care by holding insurance companies more accountable.

So Obama took the emotional and political high ground by opposing his allies, the insurers. Through political arm-twisting, Obama got his way, and on March 23, 2010, he signed the Patient Protection and Affordable Care Act.

Proponents called it a great day for American health care; opponents called it a disastrous overreach by the government.

Supreme Court Rules on Constitutionality of Affordable Care Act in 2012

After President Obama signed the Affordable Care Act, 26 states joined in a federal lawsuit challenging the constitutionality of the individual mandate and expansion of Medicaid. In addition, the National Federation of Independent Businesses also filed a lawsuit. The US Supreme Court heard the cases together during its 2012 session.

On the last day of the session, June 28, the high court ruled that the individual mandate was constitutional under the power of Congress to levy taxes.

But the court also ruled that the expansion of Medicaid called for under the Affordable Care Act was unconstitutionally coercive. The court said that the federal government could not coerce states into expanding their Medicaid programs by threatening to cut off existing funding for Medicaid.

Thus, the court opened the door for states to opt out of a major provision in the Affordable Care Act and not expand their Medicaid programs. Some governors have said their states will opt out of the Medicaid expansion, but whether that occurs is yet to be seen. The expansion of Medicaid eligibility standards is scheduled to start in 2014, and there is no deadline for states to declare their participation.

Meanwhile, as of this writing, the country was in a heated and tight race for the presidency. Mitt Romney, the Republican nominee, has said that he would repeal what he calls "Obamacare" on his first day in office. Whether he can or not is something we'll go into in a later chapter, but the subject of health care is a major political issue in 2012.

Health Care Reform Summary, Schedule

The new health care law is expansive in scope and ambitious in goals. It affects consumers, insurers, employers, health care providers, hospitals, nursing homes, Medicare and Medicaid beneficiaries, drug companies, medical-device makers, and government officials. Its timeline for full implementation runs ten years, through 2019.

While some aspects of the bill were initiated in 2010, the most dramatic changes are scheduled between 2014 and 2016. All this will be done in the face of stiff political opposition.

HEALTH CARE REFORM GLOSSARY

The following are a few terms that may help people understand health care reform.

Federal poverty level: The US government definition of poverty used to calculate eligibility for benefits and programs. The poverty level for 2012 was $11,170 for an individual and $23,050 for a family of four. It is slightly higher for Alaska and Hawaii.

Premium: The amount paid, often monthly, for health insurance. The cost of the premium may be shared between employers or government purchasers and individuals.

Premium assistance tax credit or premium subsidy: A refundable tax credit a person or family can use to help purchase insurance through an exchange. The amount is calculated on a sliding scale for people with incomes between 133 percent and 400 percent of the poverty level. The government can pay the credit directly to the exchange, or people can pay the premiums out of pocket and claim a credit on tax returns.

Small business tax credit: A tax credit for employers that offer insurance coverage and have fewer than 25 workers. Eligibility depends on the number of employees and the amount they earn, along with the amount subsidized by the employer.

The big goal of health care reform is to substantially reduce the 50 million–plus Americans who are now uninsured. According to the Congressional Budget Office, by 2019 the new law will extend medical coverage to an additional 32 million Americans—roughly the population of Canada.

The government hopes to accomplish this by expanding the nation's public/private insurance system. That would drive the nation's rate of uninsured people down to 8 percent, instead of a projected 19 percent if health care reform had not been enacted.

In brief, the new health care law includes the following initiatives:

- *Internet-based exchanges established in each state.* It allows consumers and businesses to comparison shop for policies. Rates will be kept affordable through competition and tax credits for people with income up to four times the poverty level.

- *Significant new prohibitions and requirements that target the health insurance industry.* Insurers will face regulations telling them who they must offer coverage to, how much they can charge, how much they can spend on administrative costs, how much their customers can pay in out-of-pocket costs, how to describe their policies, and the type of care their policies must include.

- *Most large employers must provide insurance to workers, or face penalties.* Smaller employers are exempt from the rule, but tax incentives are being offered to encourage some smaller employers to provide insurance to workers.

- *Virtually all Americans must have minimum insurance coverage by 2014, or face tax penalties.* People who can't find affordable coverage are exempted from this individual mandate. There are also tax subsidies to help pay premiums.

- *Government changes in how it pays for care and the type of care it accepts as adequate.* Providers will be rewarded for good quality of care, and penalized for avoidable medical problems. The new law places more emphasis on primary care and preventive care, and calls for more medical care that is based upon scientific evidence of effectiveness.

THE COST AND WHO PAYS FOR REFORM

The cost of the Patient Protection and Affordable Care Act of 2010 is estimated at $1.1 trillion from 2012 to 2021, according to the Congressional Budget Office. That's about $3,500 for every man, woman, and child in America.

At one point, the budget office estimated that the new law would reduce the budget deficit, but rising costs of coverage provisions and a slow economy reversed that. In its March 13, 2012, estimate, the budget office calculated that budget deficits caused by health care reform would average about $150 billion a year over the ten-year period.

But it's doubtful those numbers will hold steady. Much of the expense for health care reform comes from expanding Medicaid. That is expected to cost $1.5 trillion over ten years, but the Supreme Court ruled in 2012 that states were not required to expand their Medicaid programs. If states decide to opt out of the Medicaid expansion—as some have said they will—that could have a big impact on the cost of health care reform.

Also, some savings were expected to come from changes to the Medicare program. Under the new law, the government wanted to cut payments to Medicare Advantage plans and some providers. It created a new Independent Payment Advisory Board charged with limiting overall growth in Medicare spending. However, cuts to Medicare Advantage plans proved to be politically unpopular, and the government offset cuts with a bonus plan for quality improvement. There is political pressure to disband the Independent Payment Advisory Board before it has even started work.

To raise revenue for reform, new taxes are planned for health insurers, drug companies, medical device makers, and indoor tanning businesses. Tax penalties will be assessed in 2014 against people who fail to purchase minimum coverage.

On January 1, 2013, higher income earners—individuals making more than $200,000 and couples making more than $250,000—will face an increase in Medicare taxes on earnings and a new Medicare tax on unearned income. In 2018, people with high cost, or "Cadillac," insurance plans will be subject to a new tax.

Individual Mandate, Tax Penalties Scheduled for 2014

Perhaps the most controversial aspect of health care reform is the individual mandate, or requirement that nearly all US citizens and legal residents have minimum medical coverage beginning in 2014.

Many authorities believe the mandate is essential to health care reform because without it, some people may choose not to purchase insurance until they become sick. That would drive up premiums for everyone else. Opponents of the mandate claimed the federal government lacked constitutional authority to impose such an overarching requirement, and several states challenged the mandate in federal courts. The Supreme Court, however, upheld the mandate as something the federal government could do under its taxation powers.

There are several exemptions from the mandate. The penalties, which are enforced through the federal income tax system, are generally less than the cost of purchasing insurance for many people. Tax credits will be available for lower-income people who purchase insurance through exchanges.

Penalties will be phased in over three years. They hit their maximum in 2016, requiring those without coverage to pay the greater of $695 per uninsured person ($2,085 maximum per family) or 2.5 percent a family's income.

In 2014, those without insurance coverage will pay the greater of $95 per person ($285 maximum per family) or 1 percent of taxable income, and in

2015, those without insurance will pay the greater of $325 per person ($975 maximum per family) or 2 percent of taxable income.

Exemptions may be granted for religious objections or financial hardship, and to Native Americans, undocumented immigrants, jail and prison inmates, those without coverage for less than three months, people for whom the cost of minimum coverage would exceed 8 percent of income, and people with incomes below the tax-filing threshold.

Tax credits to help pay for insurance purchased through exchanges will be available in 2014 to individuals and families with income between 133 percent and 400 percent of the federal poverty level. (The poverty level in 2011 was $10,890 for an individual and $22,350 for a family of four.)

Businesses Face New Rules for Covering Workers

Starting January 1, 2014, the new health care law requires larger employers to offer insurance coverage to workers. The law sets standards for the value of the benefit, and tax penalties for failure to comply. Employers with fewer than 50 workers are exempt.

For example, an employer with more than 50 workers that *does not* offer health insurance—and has at least one full-time worker who receives a premium tax credit—will face a tax penalty of $2,000 per worker. However, the first 30 workers are excluded from the penalty assessment.

For an employer with more than 50 workers that *does* offer health insurance but the benefit is so low that at least one employee receives a premium tax credit through an exchange, the penalty could amount to the lesser of $3,000 for each worker receiving a premium tax credit, or $2,000 for each full-time employee.

An employer with more than 50 workers that does offer coverage must also offer certain workers free-choice vouchers that they can take to an exchange to get coverage, including premium tax credits. In turn, employers can avoid penalties for the workers who receive tax credit through exchanges. To get these vouchers, workers must have incomes less than 400 percent of the federal poverty level and their share of the workplace premium would fall between 8 percent and 9.8 percent of their income. The voucher amount would be equal to what the employer would have paid for the worker's coverage.

To encourage them to offer health plans, another type of tax credit will be available for some of the nation's smallest employers. In addition, separate exchanges will be established to allow small businesses to purchase coverage for their workers.

Medicaid Beneficiaries Could Expand by 16 Million

Under health care reform, Medicaid, the public insurance program for the poor, was expected to increase by about 16 million beneficiaries after eligibility requirements are loosened in 2014.

States operate Medicaid programs with the federal government providing most funding, and they now set their own rules for eligibility. The federal government planned to make the income eligibility requirement consistent nationally in 2014. However, the Supreme Court ruled in 2012 that states could maintain existing federal funding for Medicaid without expanding the program or changing eligibility standards.

For states that do decide to expand Medicaid, the new rule will require them to offer the coverage to all people earning up to 133 percent of the poverty level.

Additionally, most states have been denying eligibility to adults without dependent children, regardless of income. For states that decide to expand their Medicaid programs, the new health care law will require them to accept adults without children into the program if they meet income requirements.

Private Insurance to Expand by 16 Million Policyholders

Private insurance coverage is expected to grow by 16 million policyholders, mostly through the 2014 creation of new state-based marketplaces or exchanges.

These exchanges will allow consumers to comparison shop. Moreover, to ensure that premiums are affordable, the government will offer tax credits to people with incomes up to 400 percent of the poverty level.

Other private insurance growth is expected because of new rules that allow children up to 26 years old to stay on their parents' policies. The children don't have to live in their parents' home or be in college, but the coverage will not extend to their spouses or children.

Growth will also be driven by the new rule keeping insurers from withholding policies from customers because they are sick, or canceling policies because they have exceeded annual or lifetime limits.

Push for More Preventive Care and Better Quality

Health care reform will attempt to shift more focus to preventive care, better quality care, and care that is more effective. Much of the responsibility for overseeing and implementing these fundamental changes in health care will fall upon insurers, doctors, and hospitals.

For policies issued after September 23, 2013, the new health care law requires that insurers provide a long list of preventive procedures that must be delivered with no out-of-pocket costs to policyholders.

These procedures include cholesterol checks, colorectal cancer screening for people over 50, HIV screening for all adults in high-risk groups, depression screening for adults, obesity screening and counseling for adults, tobacco screening for adults, and intervention for tobacco users.

States will be given enhanced Medicaid payments if they include these preventive services in their plans.

The new law increases payments to Medicare and Medicaid primary care providers, and provides incentives for new doctors and other health professionals to practice primary care.

Health care reform creates the Prevention and Public Health Fund with money that will be used for preventing diseases and conditions such as HIV and obesity, and proving tobacco cessation support while strengthening the nation's public health system.

The new law will attempt to improve the quality of health care by developing a national strategy. Included in this strategy is the creation of medical homes—a health care setting where patients receive primary care and have an ongoing relationship with a provider who coordinates their care. The government would hold providers more accountable for care dispensed through these "homes."

With health care reform, payments to providers will be based on quality measures. Quality of care information will be provided to patients so that they can make informed decisions about choosing where to go for care.

The government will exert financial pressure on providers to use treatments that have been proven through scientific research to be the most effective. There will also be financial penalties for hospitals where preventable conditions such as infections and readmissions persist.

Twenty-three Million Americans Expected to Remain Uninsured

Despite all the changes to health care, the Congressional Budget Office estimates that 23 million people living in America will remain uninsured by 2019, and it could be more than that if some states decide to opt out of expanding their Medicaid programs.

The uninsured will include undocumented immigrants who are not legal residents and therefore will not be eligible for Medicaid or premium subsidies. Also, there is always a significant group of people who—although eligible for Medicaid—won't enroll.

Some people will be given exemptions from the individual mandate. Some people will choose to pay the penalty rather than getting insured.

And many of the remaining uninsured people will have low incomes and not be able to afford care. Therefore, the nation must still maintain a system of "safety net" health care providers.

Timeline for Health Care Reform Provisions

There are more than 90 major provisions in the Patient Protection and Affordable Care Act of 2010. The changes started in 2010, and run through 2019. The significant changes occur in the first half of the decade. The following timeline highlights many of the provisions occurring from 2010 through 2014.

2010	Insurance premium rate reviews; changes in Medicare provider rates; Prevention and Public Health Fund; Medicare beneficiary drug rebate; Medicaid coverage for childless adults; consumer web site; tax on indoor tanning services; adult dependant coverage to age 26; consumer protections in insurance; preventive benefits in new health insurance plans; and temporary exchanges for people with pre-existing conditions.
2011	Limits on administrative costs for insurers; closing Medicare drug coverage gap; Medicare preventive benefits; start of phased cuts to Medicare Advantage plans; changes to tax-free savings accounts; Medicaid penalties for hospital-acquired infections; and Medicare Independent Payment Advisory Board.
2012	Increased fraud and abuse prevention for Medicaid and Medicare; new annual fees on pharmaceutical industry; and financial penalties from Medicare for hospitals making preventable readmissions.

2013	Increased Medicaid payment for states offering preventive services; states report intent to operate exchanges; increased Medicaid payments for primary care; increased threshold for itemizing medical expenses; new limits on flexible medical savings accounts; Medicare tax increase for high incomes; employer retiree coverage subsidy; and excise tax on medical devices.
2014	Health insurance exchanges; individual mandate requiring insurance; free-choice vouchers from employers; expanded Medicaid eligibility; tax credits to subsidize premiums; guaranteed availability of insurance; no annual limits on coverage; essential health benefits package; penalties for employers failing to meet regulations for coverage; new fees on health insurance industry; and reductions in Medicare payment for hospital-acquired infections.

Coming Next

The next chapter deals with portions of the new health care law that have been enacted early, mostly in 2010. You know, some of the most dreaded words in the American lexicon are: "We're from the government, and we're here to help." Well, some of the changes may have actually helped, but others are requiring more work.

Early Changes

Health Care Reform's First Ups, Downs

Some aspects of the Patient Protection and Affordable Care Act of 2010 started like a stumble-rama. For example:

- The new health care law in 2010 created temporary insurance exchanges. These exchanges were established nationwide to sell policies to people with pre-existing conditions who were having difficulty getting coverage from private insurers. A government actuary predicted 375,000 enrollees would pour into the exchanges by the end of the year. Only 12,000 people enrolled. Officials blamed lack of awareness and rates that were too high. They staged a publicity campaign, and lowered rates. Enrollment rose to 50,000.

- Another early element of the law prohibited health insurance companies from turning away children with pre-existing medical conditions. In response, major insurers were driven by financial fears to completely stop selling policies that just covered children.

- And still another early reform gave the government power to review insurance rate increases of more than 10 percent. What most people failed to realize is that the law made little provision for doing anything about excessive rate hikes, other than look at them, and many states were incapable of even doing that.

Nonetheless, other early elements of the new law were more successful and popular:

- More than 3.2 million Medicare beneficiaries got $250 rebate checks from the government. These beneficiaries had fallen into a "donut hole," or coverage gap, in the Medicare Part D drug plan. This one-time rebate is accompanied by a 50 percent discount on brand-name prescription drugs until the donut hole closes in 2020.

- Additionally, in 2010, the new health care law allowed young adults to stay on their parents' insurance policies until age 26. The change was supposed to go into effect on September 23, 2010. But Kathleen Sebelius, Secretary of the US Department of Health and Human Services (HHS), asked insurers to begin early so young adults could avoid being dropped from policies, and then have to re-enroll. Dozens of insurers, including some of the nation's largest, complied.

And the new health care law restricted the insurance industry's ability to cancel policies when patients become ill, and prohibited lifetime limits on health policies. Let's take a look a closer look at some of these early provisions of health care reform from 2010 until 2012. We'll sort out details, and see what the law was intended to do and what it was really doing.

Temporary Exchanges for People with High-Risk Conditions

The Pre-Existing Condition Insurance Plan was conceived to bridge coverage for people who had been denied private insurance because of health problems.

These high-risk exchanges were established in 2010, but will be unnecessary after 2014 when the new law makes it illegal for insurers to turn away customers with pre-existing conditions. High-risk customers may then get insurance through a network of permanent exchanges set up for everybody.

Enrollment at temporary exchanges was dismally low when they first opened. A Medicaid actuary had predicted that hundreds of thousands of people would turn out, but only a few thousand did. Officials blamed a lack of public awareness along with rates and deductibles that were too high. Officials made adjustments, and enrollment picked up, although it never came anywhere near the original estimates.

Insurance sold through these temporary exchanges offer typical coverage, including primary care, specialty care, hospital care, and prescription medications. There is no waiting period for coverage, unlike the old high-risk pools that were run by many states.

Qualifying is simple. People must be:

- Denied regular insurance coverage because of a pre-existing condition.

- A US citizen or residing in the country legally.

- Uninsured for at least six months. People don't qualify if they have insurance—even if it excludes their pre-existing medical condition—or are enrolled in one of the high-risk insurance pools operated by a state.

Some of these temporary exchanges are operated by states, and some are operated by the federal government. The program is available for people in all states. For automatic direction to your appropriate web site, go to the Pre-Existing Condition Insurance Plan web site at www.pcip.gov.

▨ **Caution**   The government warns people that it is unnecessary to pay anybody a fee to enroll in high-risk exchanges created under the Pre-Existing Condition Insurance Plan. The US Department of Health and Human Services notified state insurance commissioners in September 2010 that sale representatives were peddling fraudulent policies door-to-door and via toll-free numbers nationwide. The representatives claimed the policies were part of health care reform. Targets of this type of insurance fraud are typically asked to pay a "membership fee" to a non-existent union or association. There is no fee for signing up with exchange-based plans. Contact the exchange center directly through www.pcip.gov, or call 1-866-717-5826 (TTY: 1-866-561-1604).

Expanded Plan Options in 2011 for High-Risk Exchanges

People who enrolled in the temporary exchanges when they first opened in 2010 had one choice, a Standard Plan. Starting in 2011, officials expanded the selection to three options: the Standard Plan, the Extended Plan, and the Health Savings Account–eligible plan. A child-only rate was added, too, as many private insurers stopped issuing those types of policies as health care reform was enacted.

Each plan offers preventive care with no deductibles if policyholders see an in-network doctor. There are deductibles for other medical services, and policyholders must pay 20 percent of remaining in-network medical costs. Deductibles are higher for out-of-network care, and policyholders must pay

40 percent of those costs. The amount that a policyholder must pay is capped at a "catastrophic maximum," which was between $4,000 and $7,000 a month in 2012, depending on the plan.

Table 2-1 shows a sample of rates from three plans offered through a temporary exchange set up in Tennessee and serving some Southern states.

Table 2-1. Monthly Rates for Pre-Existing Condition Insurance Plans* (Alabama sample)

Age	Standard Option	Extended Option	HSA Option
0 to 18	$110	$148	$114
19 to 34	$164	$221	$170
35 to 44	$197	$265	$205
45 to 54	$251	$338	$262
55-plus	$350	$471	$364

*Shows July 2011 individual adult rates (in Alabama) for coverage through a temporary exchange established for people with pre-existing health conditions.

The following briefly details the three plan options.

- *Standard Plan*: This plan has a $2,000 in-network medical deductible and $3,000 out-of-network medical deductable. It also has a separate $500 formulary drug deductible and a $750 non-formulary drug deductible. It offers lower premiums.

- *Extended Plan*: This plan has a $1,000 in-network medical deductible and a $1,500 out-of-network medical deductible. It also has a separate $250 formulary drug deductible and a $375 non-formulary drug deductible. The premiums are slightly higher than the standard plan.

- *Health Savings Account Option*: This option carries a $2,500 in-network medical deductible and $3,000 out-of-network medical deductible. There are no drug deductibles. Premiums are fairly low. The plan works through the existing health savings account system, which provides favorable tax treatment.

PRE-EXISTING CONDITIONS EXIST IN ABUNDANCE

The term "pre-existing condition" gets tossed around a lot in health care reform, and it seems simple enough: a serious medical condition.

But a pre-existing condition may be a little less serious, and a lot more common than many people think. A government analysis released in January 2011 concluded that 129 million Americans, or about 40 percent of the population, have some sort of medical, or pre-existing, condition, which is a red flag for insurers.

Pre-existing conditions can include health problems as serious as lung cancer, but also as controllable as high blood pressure. About 75 million Americans have high blood pressure, or hypertension, which if left uncontrolled can kill, often through strokes and heart or kidney failure. But high blood pressure can usually be controlled with medications—including some that cost about a dime a day.

There are more than 100 pre-existing mental and physical conditions that insurers may use to deny coverage. Some of the more common ones include AIDS, alcohol abuse, asthma, bipolar disorders, heart diseases, kidney diseases, diabetes, obesity, and smoking.

New Insurance Guarantees for Children with Health Issues

On June 28, 2010, the government issued regulations prohibiting insurers from excluding children under age 19 from coverage because of pre-existing conditions. The law applies to some existing group and individual health policies, and most new health policies.

In response, scores of insurers in 34 states stopped offering child-only policies out of financial fears. Some states took regulatory action to encourage insurers to keep offering child-only coverage, and began considering legislation that would require insurers that offered family coverage to also offer child-only policies.

In September 2010, HHS Secretary Kathleen Sebelius wrote the Blue Cross and Blue Shield Association to express her concern about emerging difficulties with insuring children: "It appears that some of your members are now turning a blind eye and declining to sell child-only policies in lieu of offering coverage to children with pre-existing conditions."

Getting insurance for a child with a pre-existing health condition can be difficult and expensive if coverage is unavailable through a parent's workplace or a public program like Medicaid's Children's Health Insurance Program (CHIP).

And there are many millions of these children. For example, about 9 percent of all children have asthma problems, and almost 14 percent have special health care needs, according to the 2005–2006 National Survey of Children with Special Health Care Needs.

Sebelius pleaded with insurers to offer the coverage to desperate families, and offered clarifications to the new regulations that might encourage them to do so—things like waiving the new regulations for some existing, or "grandfathered," plans or increasing their rates as allowed under state laws.

She also said the Obama Administration was finding ways to provide more coverage to affected families. The avenues being considered by the federal government to fill the gap included employer-based family plans, Medicaid's CHIP, and temporary exchanges set up under the Pre-Existing Condition Insurance Plan.

"ADVERSE SELECTION" AND AVOIDING CUSTOMERS WORTH AVOIDING

There's a phenomenon called *adverse selection* that is well known to insurers. It came into play when the new health care law required them to cover children regardless of pre-existing conditions.

Adverse selection means that people with the highest potential to file claims are people who are most likely to seek, obtain, and use health insurance.

It's common sense. If you know your health or your child's health is bad, you want insurance. That gets expensive for insurers. They want customers who file few claims, and they have a tendency to turn down customers who run up big medical costs.

It's kind of the opposite of Groucho Marx's old line: "I wouldn't want to join any club that would have me as a member." With insurers, the more you want to be a member of their club, the less they want you.

Young Adults Get Extension to Age 26 on Parents' Policies

For years, young adults have been a group of Americans with one of the highest rates of being uninsured, about 30 percent. They often hold entry-level or part-time jobs that offer few benefits.

Many people believe that young adults don't really need insurance since they're so healthy, but studies have shown that one in six has a chronic disease and about half have problems paying medical bills.

Figure 2-1 provides data in chart form that shows some of the difficulties young adults have encountered with getting good insurance and paying medical bills in recent years.

Two-Thirds of Uninsured Young Adults Had Cost-Related Access Problems in the Past Year, Compared with One-Third of Those Who Were Insured All Year

Percent of adults ages 19–29 reporting the following problems in the past year because of cost:

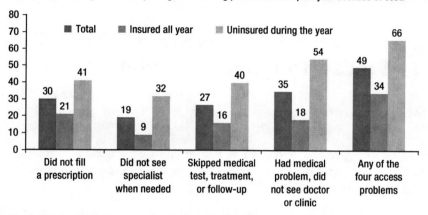

Source: The Commonwealth Fund Biennial Health Insurance Survey (2007).

Figure 2-1. Contrary to popular belief, young people have had plenty of difficulty getting health insurance and care. Source: Commonwealth Fund.

Another early provision of the Patient Protection and Affordable Care Act of 2010 allowed young adults up to age 26 to stay on their parents' insurance policies. The government estimated that the provision would extend coverage to 1.2 million young adults and increase premiums by less than 1 percent over the long run.

After September 23, 2010, the new law required plans that offered dependent coverage to extend coverage to children up to age 26, at the same price normally paid for dependents. The children neither have to live with parents nor do they have to be claimed by their parents as a dependent for tax purpose. But the coverage does not extend to the dependent's children or spouses. Also, if a dependent has access to insurance through an employer, his parents' insurer may deny him coverage. That rule changes in 2014 when a dependent may opt to stay on a parent's policy to age 26, regardless of other coverage offered through a workplace.

Many insurers began offering coverage to uninsured, older dependents early to prevent them from dropping from parents' policies and then having to enroll again. The US Department of Treasury also issued guidance saying that the value of this benefit is non-taxable.

The National Health Interview Survey found that as of December 2011, an additional 3.1 million young Americans had gained health insurance coverage because of the provision.

There is an exception. Group plans that are "grandfathered" are not required to offer extended dependent coverage if a youth is eligible for group coverage outside the parent's plan.

Insurance-Rate Reviews Start, Some States Toughen Oversight

Just after he signed the Patient Protection and Affordable Care Act of 2010, President Obama warned insurance executives that rate increases would be carefully monitored, beginning in 2011.

But the law didn't give the government authority to do anything about rate hikes. Enforcement was largely dependent upon transparency to shame insurers into doing the right thing.

The day before Obama's warning, the Kaiser Family Foundation reported that premiums for individual policies increased in recent months by an average of 20 percent.

Some insurers, like Regence Blue Shield in the state of Washington, blamed health care reform for increases. Regence stopped offering child-only policies and raised 2011 premiums for some policyholders by 37 percent.

Health care reform did give regulators one tool that could be used in a roundabout way to hold down rate increases. Under the new law, starting in 2011, insurers must spend either 80 or 85 percent of money earned from premiums on actual health care services for policyholders. If this requirement isn't met, insurers must give policyholders a rebate in 2012 (which some did).

Meanwhile, Congress and some state Legislatures have been working on new measures to put more teeth into the provision allowing oversight of insurance premium increases. Moreover, the federal government has been helping some states review rate increases since many didn't have systems in place for before health care reform.

In August of 2010, the HHS began awarding millions of dollars in grants so that states could improve the processes for reviewing rate increases. As of

February 16, 2012, all but 12 states had effective rate review programs in place. According the HHS Center for Consumer Information & Insurance Oversight, the states that still relied upon varying levels of federal assistance were Alabama, Arizona, Idaho, Louisiana, Missouri, Montana, North Carolina, Oregon, Virginia, Washington, Wisconsin, and Wyoming.

Workers Hit, Too

Health care premiums have been increasing for decades. In recent years, not only have premiums increased, but employers have also decreased subsidies for workers' policies. Figure 2-2 illustrates the problem.

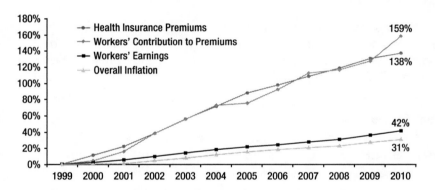

Cumulative Changes in Health Insurance Premiums, Workers' Contribution to Premiums, Inflation, and Workers' Earnings, 1999–2010

Source: Kaiser Slides, The Henry J. Kaiser Family Foundation and HRET, September 2010

Figure 2-2. Insurance premiums are increasing faster than wages, and employers are paying less of the cost. Source: This information was reprinted with permission from the Henry J. Kaiser Family Foundation.

Insurers Banned from Cutting and Capping Coverage

The government issued new rules in June 2010 to discourage insurers from rescinding coverage and to ban them from placing lifetime limits on policies. The rules also started phasing out annual limits on policies, and gave patients more leeway in seeking emergency care.

In the past, some policyholders paid premiums for years, and when they encountered an expensive medical problem, they had policies rescinded, or canceled, for minor errors made when first applying for insurance. A congressional investigation found that over a three-year period, insurers had rescinded 20,000 policies at an estimated savings of $300 million.

Under the new health care law, insurers can no longer rescind coverage of policyholders except in cases of substantive fraud or intentional misrepresentation on an application for coverage. If insurers think they have good reason for canceling coverage, they must give policyholders 30 days' notice of termination, and make an appeals process available.

The new rules also stop insurers from placing lifetime limits on the amount of coverage their policies provide. The new regulations are phasing out annual limits that insurers sometimes put on coverage. The limits were set at $750,000 in 2010 and rise to $2 million by 2013. All annual limits will be prohibited in 2014.

In 2010, new policies were required to have a process that allows consumers to appeal insurance company decisions to an external party.

Policyholders no longer must seek prior authorization from an insurer before seeking emergency services either in or out of a plan's network. And if a policyholder gets emergency care out of system, the benefits have to be equal to those provided in the system.

■ **Caution**   There are warnings for policyholders going out-of-network for emergency services. Out-of-system providers may bill patients for costs not covered by policies. However, there are some limits as to what providers can charge in these circumstances. New rules for emergency-care access may not apply to old or "grandfathered" policies.

Slowly Filling Medicare's Prescription Drug "Donut Hole"

When the government set up the Medicare Part D drug benefit in 2006, a "donut hole," or gap in coverage, was inserted to save the plan money—but it cost beneficiaries plenty.

In 2010, a beneficiary hit the dreaded donut hole after spending $940 out of pocket on drugs, and didn't leave it until spending $4,550. Table 2-2 briefly details the donut hole.

Table 2-2. Targeting the Donut Hole* in Medicare Part D

For drugs costing between...	Medicare Part D beneficiaries pay...	Total cost to beneficiaries...
$0 and $310	100% up to $310	$0 to $310
$310 to $2,830	25% up to $630	$310 to $940
DONUT HOLE $2,830 and $6,440	$940 plus 100% of total costs over $2,830	$940 to $4,550
Over $6,440	5% up to no limit	$4,550 plus 5% over $6,440

*The so-called "donut hole" in Medicare's prescription drug plan for 2010. The donut hole is the part of coverage where beneficiaries pay ALL the costs in that range. It is between $2,830 and $6,440, and is $3,610 wide.

About 3.9 million Part D enrollees hit the donut hole in 2009. While in the donut hole, their out-of-pocket spending for brand-name drugs hit $3.6 billion and $800 million for generic drugs.

The new health care law gradually eliminates the donut hole while, in the meantime, providing rebates and discounts for Medicare Part D beneficiaries who hit this gap in coverage.

In 2010, Part D enrollees got a $250 rebate if they had any out-of-pocket spending in the gap. In 2011, Part D enrollees began receiving a 50 percent discount on brand-name drugs purchased in the coverage gap.

Medicare is gradually phasing in more subsidies for brand-name and generic drugs purchased in the gap, and reducing the current co-pay from 100 percent to 25 percent by 2020.

Changes Continued Throughout 2011

The Affordable Care Act continued to implement a host of smaller but important changes throughout 2011. They included:

- The "medical loss ratio" rule that requires health plans spend a specific proportion of premium dollars for actual medical care of policyholders. The amount required was set at 85 percent for large group markets and 80 percent for small group markets. Some states, however, have received waivers for this rule.

- A 10 percent bonus for primary care doctors providing services to Medicare beneficiaries, and surgeons practicing in areas where there is a shortage of health professionals.

- The establishment of an Independent Payment Advisory Board for Medicare. In 2014, this 15-member board is expected to make its first recommendations on ways to reduce growth rates in Medicare spending.

Coming Next

This chapter covered most major early changes to health care reform implemented up to 2012. There are two notable omissions: the new tax on tanning salons, which is covered in Chapter 10, and the tax break for small businesses that provide insurance, which is covered in Chapter 4. In the next chapter, we will start looking at how the new health care law will affect individuals and families in the long run.

Some states have set up prototypes for insurance exchanges, or have created actual exchanges. We will see how those work. We will also look at how people can keep their existing health insurance policies, and at how health care reform will affect income tax deductions in coming years.

New Choices

Individual, Family Insurance Options

Health care reform means big changes in the relationships individuals and families have with insurers. Health care reform may change where people purchase insurance and how much they pay for it. It will require them to have insurance, and it will change what is covered by policies. It changes how tax laws treat medical expenses. And it provides a multitude of protections intended to keep insurers fair, honest, and efficient.

Remember President Obama's promise: "If you like your health plan, you can keep it. ... Nobody is talking about taking that away from you." The new health care law attempts to keep that promise—sort of.

This chapter looks at how the new law allows for grandfathering existing policies; how the new law compels people to buy insurance; and tax consequences of the new law. It also covers setting up insurance exchanges and the Massachusetts experiment in health care reform.

Some Policies May Be "Grandfathered" Under New Law

Under health care reform, it is possible for individuals and families to keep existing insurance plans, but the circumstances must be just right. Plans must be "grandfathered" into the new system, but that's not being done for all plans.

▨ **Caution** Grandfathering policies will be largely left up to insurers, and many have already decided not to treat any plans this way because of administrative costs. Ask your insurer if your plan is being grandfathered.

To be grandfathered, the plan must exist before March 23, 2010, and must essentially leave benefits and co-pays intact. Plans lose their grandfather status if there are substantial cuts to services or increased out-of-pocket costs for policyholders. Plans created after March 23, 2010, are considered new, and can't be grandfathered.

Grandfathered plans must incorporate some consumer protections enacted through health care reform. As of September 23, 2010, they include the following:

- Coverage of dependents up to age 26
- No lifetime dollar limits
- Limited annual dollar limits
- No exclusions for children under age 19 who have pre-existing health conditions
- No rescission of policies, or retroactively dropping coverage when someone gets sick

In 2011, grandfathered plans fell under health care reform's provision requiring insurers to spend 80 to 85 percent of revenue from premiums on actual health care. If this so-called "medical loss ratio" requirement isn't met, insurers must give policyholders a rebate.

In 2014, grandfathered plans, like all insurance plans, can no longer exclude members for pre-existing conditions. There can be no waiting periods for coverage longer than 90 days. There will be no annual dollar limits.

Grandfathered plans will *not* have to incorporate the following elements of health care reform:

- Preventive care with no co-pays
- Internal appeals and external review over disputed claims
- The right to choose your own in-network primary care doctor or pediatrician
- OB/GYN visits without referrals
- Out-of-network emergency room services without prior authorization or higher co-pay
- Coverage for routine care in an approved clinical trial
- Small-group policy coverage without medical underwriting
- Guaranteed renewability of coverage

MINI-MED PLANS GET WAIVERS FOR COVERAGE CAPS

In addition to grandfathered plans, another important exception to the new health care law emerged in 2010.

Some limited benefit plans, called mini-meds, have very low annual caps on coverage—often $2,000 to $10,000—and were being issued one-year waivers by the government in late 2010. The waivers allowed dozens of insurers to continue offering these plans without the $750,000 a year cap prescribed by the new health care law.

The issue surfaced publicly when fast-food giant McDonald's sent a memo to the government saying it might be unaffordable to continue insuring its 30,000 workers if mini-med policies had to meet annual caps. McDonald's covers its workers through a for-profit insurer owned by Blue Cross Blue Shield plans.

Fearing a massive loss of coverage—no matter how limited—government planners issued a waiver on annual limits. The government also issued one-year waivers to at least 30 other insurers, including Cigna and Aetna, allowing them to continuing selling policies with low caps on coverage.

There is much dispute among officials about doing this. Plans that cap coverage at a few thousand dollars provide no protection against catastrophic loss. But, officials are concerned that creating too much turmoil in the insurance marketplace while health care reform is being enacted could do more harm than good.

Other standards set by health care reform are impossible for mini-meds to meet, and the government is trying to make accommodations. The following table shows the extreme limits that often accompany mini-med insurance plans, like the one offered by McDonald's (information taken from a 2010 McDonald's benefit handout that shows the company's mini-med plans, premiums, and annual limits). There was no provision in health care reform for these plans.

McDonald's Mini-Med Insurance Plans

Type of Plan	Weekly Premium	Annual Premium	Maximum Annual Benefit
Basic	$13.99	$727.48	$2,000
Medium	$24.30	$1,263.60	$5,000
Higher	$32.30	$1,679.60	$10,000
Source: Balloon-Juice.com and *The Wall Street Journal*.			

The following lists what the McDonald's plans pay for, up to the annual maximum:

- 100 percent of visits to primary care doctor or specialist doctors, after a $20 co-pay.

- 100 percent of prescription drug costs, after a $5 co-pay for generic and a $50 co-pay for brand-name drugs.

- 70 percent of inpatient hospital care.

Insurance Exchanges Are Critical to Health Care Reform

A nationwide network of insurance exchanges will be a key element in determining the ultimate success or failure of health care reform.

Known as American Health Benefit Exchanges, these state-based organizations will provide one-stop, competitive insurance plan shopping on the Internet. People will be able to compare and purchase insurance plans while learning about possible subsidies and tax incentives.

Small businesses employing up to 100 workers may also use the exchanges to pool buying-power and lower administrative costs.

Many people are expected to purchase insurance policies through these exchanges, but many people are also expected to continue purchasing insurance through the workplace or the private market. The Congressional Budget Office estimates that by 2019, about 28 million Americans will purchase health insurance through exchanges.

States are being encouraged to create and operate exchanges, but if they don't, the federal government will fill the gap. States such as California, Maryland, and Colorado were the first to receive federal grants. By March 2012, thirteen states and the District of Columbia had actually established exchanges. Federal funding will be available until 2015 to establish these exchanges, and then they must become self-sustaining.

More than one exchange may be set up in a state, but exchanges must serve a distinct geographical area and not overlap. In some areas, states are being allowed to cooperate in creating exchanges.

Exchanges must offer at least four levels of coverage with different limitations on out-of-pocket costs, as follows:

- Bronze, which will cover 60 percent of costs

- Silver, which will cover 70 percent of costs

- Gold, which will cover 80 percent of costs

- Platinum, which will cover 90 percent of costs

In addition, exchanges must offer a catastrophic coverage plan for people under age 30. Private health insurance companies that sell policies through exchanges must offer at least one plan at each level of coverage.

States may also create a Basic Health Plan for uninsured people with incomes between 133 percent and 200 percent of the poverty level. Individuals could choose this plan instead of going to an exchange and receiving premium subsidies.

Note Rates and plans offered by exchanges will depend largely upon boards or commissions established to oversee them as government agencies or non-profit organizations. Exchanges must operate within a budget, establish rules preventing fraud and waste, and operate a consumer-assistance system, including a call center.

Plans offered by exchanges must include "essential health benefits" as defined by the federal government. These benefits include the following:

- Ambulatory patient services

- Emergency services

- Hospitalization

- Maternity and newborn care

- Mental health benefits and services for substance use disorders

- Prescription drugs

- Rehabilitative services and devices

- Laboratory services

- Preventive and wellness services

- Chronic disease management

- Pediatric services, including oral and vision care

The new health care law places caps on how much money people can spend out of their own pockets for health care services included in this "essential health benefits" package.

The out-of-pocket spending caps will follow a sliding scale; people with lower incomes will pay less out of pocket than people with higher incomes.

The law ties the level of these caps to the annual out-of-pocket spending limits for high-deductible health plans associated with Health Savings Accounts. In 2012, those limits are $5,950 for individuals and $11,900 for families.

For families with incomes below 400 percent of the poverty level and who purchase coverage through an exchange, the caps will be reduced as follows:

- One-third the limit for families with incomes between 100 and 200 percent of the poverty level.

- One-half the limit for families with incomes between 200 and 300 percent of the poverty level.

- Two-thirds the limit for families with incomes between 300 and 400 percent of the poverty level.

ABORTION COVERAGE OPTIONAL UNDER NEW LAW

States may prohibit abortion coverage in health plans offered through exchanges, but they must enact laws to do so. By late 2010, at least five states—Arizona, Louisiana, Mississippi, Missouri, and Tennessee—had elected to do so.

Exchange plans that do provide abortion coverage beyond that permitted with federal funds—to save the life of the woman and in cases of rape or incest—must create separate accounts where money can be used to help women pay for these procedures. In other words, no federal money can be used. And the exchange must offer a similar plan *without* expanded abortion services.

These abortion rules are the result of a compromise struck when health care reform was working its way through Congress.

By comparison, many workplace-based insurance plans cover abortions, but some don't, according to two studies—one by the Guttmacher Institute and the other by the Kaiser Family Foundation. The Guttmacher study in 2002 found that about 85 percent of employer-based plans covered the procedure, and the Kaiser study in 2003 found that 46 percent of workers who were insured had coverage for abortion. Health care reform should have no impact on abortion coverage outside exchanges.

Also, states have their own rules when it comes to covering abortions through Medicaid, which expands dramatically under health care reform. Basically, if a state covers the procedure, it must only spend state money, except when the life of the woman is endangered, or in cases of rape and incest.

Tax Credit and Subsidies Available at Exchanges

There are two types of assistance available at exchanges and paid by the government—tax credits and subsidies. They are available to people earning between 100 and 400 percent of the poverty level. Revenue to pay for the system comes from a variety of sources, including taxes on insurance companies, medical device makers, and pharmaceutical companies.

Subsidies lower the cost of deductibles and other forms of cost sharing. They are available to households with incomes under 250 percent of the federal poverty level. For example, families with incomes below 150 percent of the poverty level would have their deductibles reduced 80 percent.

Tax credits are used to help pay premiums. They are available through advance payments the Treasury Department makes directly to the insurance company so that people don't have to wait until they file taxes. The advance payments are reconciled when the family's tax return is calculated and filed. Tax credits are generally available to households with incomes between 100 and 400 percent of the federal poverty level. The amount of the tax credit is tied to the amount of the premium so that older Americans, who face higher premiums, get higher credits. The following are two examples the Treasury Department provided on August 12, 2011, when it issued proposed regulations for tax credits.

EXAMPLE 1: Family of four with young parents and an income of $50,000

- Income as percentage of poverty level: 224 percent
- Premium for health plan at exchange: $9,000
- Premium tax credit: $5,430
- Actual family contribution: $3,570

EXAMPLE 2: Family of four with parents between 55 and 64 years old and an income of $50,000

- Income as percentage of poverty level: 224 percent
- Premium for health plan at exchange: $14,000
- Premium tax credit: $10,430
- Actual family contribution: $3,570

Wisconsin Prototype Offers Example of Insurance Exchange

To draw a better picture of how exchanges work, let's look at one recent prototype.

By the end of 2010, Wisconsin had established a prototype for an exchange web site, but the site was taken down when Governor Scott Walker rejected implementation of health care reform and said the state would return a $38 million federal grant to establish an exchange. Nonetheless, information from the prototype is still valid and provides insight into how choice and circumstance impacts premiums. Let's look at three greatly simplified scenarios from the prototype.

The scenarios are for a family of four with a $44,100 a year income, an older couple with a $117,300 a year income, and a young woman with a $45,600 a year income. The family of four qualifies for a tax credit, which amounts to $615 a month and is figured into premiums.

In all scenarios, enrollees could choose from 15 plans provided by private insurers. For the sake of simplicity, all enrollees have set priorities for their insurance plans in the following order:

1.   High overall care

2.   High quality for existing health conditions

3.   Personal doctor included

4.   Personal hospital and clinic included

5.   Low monthly premium

6.   Low out-of-pocket expenses

7.   Good customer service

Table 3-1 shows a sample of insurance rates considering that both parents smoke, but the overall health of family members is good. Premiums include a $615 tax credit per month.

Table 3-1. Wisconsin Insurance Exchange Prototype Example for a Family of Four

Plan	Monthly premium w/ tax credit	Annual out-of-pocket expense	Quality of care rating	Customer service rating
High-deductible plan No. 1	$0	$574	B+	A-
High-deductible plan No. 2	$219	$835	A	C
HMO plan	$335	$950	A	C
PPO plan	$428	$1,920	A	C

Table 3-2 shows a sample of insurance rates for a hypothetical couple that doesn't smoke. The wife is in poor health, but the husband's health is good. They both have high blood pressure.

Table 3-2. Wisconsin Insurance Exchange Prototype Example for a 64-Year-Old Couple

Plan	Monthly premium	Annual out-of-pocket expense	Quality of care rating	Customer service rating
High-deductible plan No. 1	$864	$1,518	B+	B+
High-deductible plan No. 2	$583	$1,320	B+	C
HMO plan	$957	$1,518	B+	B+
PPO plan	$1,055	$1,518	B+	B+

Table 3-3 shows rates for a hypothetical single woman in good health.

Table 3-3. Wisconsin Insurance Exchange Prototype Example for a 27-Year-Old Woman

Plan	Monthly Premium	Annual out-of-pocket expense	Quality of care rating	Customer service rating
High-deductible	$104	$320	A	C
Catastrophic care	$45	$368	B+	B+
HMO	$119	$320	A	C
PPO	$135	$320	A	C

Get it? If enrollees want to change priorities—say lower the quality of care and increase the quality of service—then the price can go up, down, or stay the same. Push in one place, and it may pop out in another. The site included a tool that allowed users to closely compare several aspects of each plan.

The Wisconsin prototype web site offered the following three types of assistance to help lower- and moderate-income customers pay their monthly premiums:

- *Federal Tax Credit*: Under the new health care law, individuals and families may be eligible for a tax credit that will be applied to health insurance premiums. The credit is based on household size, income, and amount of premium.

- *Federal Subsidies*: These may be applied to some services and co-pays to reduce out-of-pocket expenses.

- *BadgerCare Plus*: This state program would offer low or no-cost health care to lower-income Wisconsin residents.

Massachusetts Insurance Exchange Offers Real-Life Example

The deadline for the national exchange network to go online is 2014, but Massachusetts has a well-established exchange that gives a good example on how such a system operates. The Health Connector web site is located at www.mahealthconnector.org.

Massachusetts passed statewide health care reform and launched its Connector exchange in 2006. Like federal health reform, the goal in Massachusetts was to create a system to provide affordable insurance to people without workplace coverage. And the exchange was accompanied by a mandate requiring everybody in the state to have health insurance.

The Massachusetts Connector created Commonwealth Care and Commonwealth Choice, two insurance programs. Commonwealth Care provides insurance, with a sliding scale of subsidized premiums, to adults earning up to 300 percent of the poverty level. Commonwealth Choice provides a one-stop insurance shop for people who do not qualify for premium subsidies.

■ **Note** Just a reminder: the federal poverty level for 2011 was $10,890 for an individual and $22,350 for a family of four. For 2012, it was $11,170 for an individual and $23,050 for a family of four.

Commonwealth Care offers three plans for adults who are unable to get insurance through employers, family plans, or other programs. The cost depends upon gross income and location. The plans are as follows:

- *Type 1*: For people with household incomes less than or equal to 100 percent of the federal poverty level. There are no monthly premiums or deductibles. Co-pays for prescriptions are small.

- *Type 2*: For people with household incomes between 100 percent and 200 percent of the poverty level. Monthly premiums for the lowest option in the least expensive location range from $0 to $28. There are co-pays for services and prescriptions.

- *Type 3*: For people with household incomes between 200 percent and 300 percent of the poverty level. Monthly premiums for the lowest option and least expensive location range between $78 and $138. There are co-pays for services and prescriptions.

Commonwealth Care is administered by existing insurance companies, which are chosen by bids. In 2008, about 175,000 people enrolled. Eligibility of policyholders is routinely re-evaluated.

Commonwealth Choice offers four types of plans through seven private insurance companies. All plans have premiums, and costs vary widely, depending on age, location, and type of plan. The plans are as follows:

- *Gold plans*: Higher monthly premiums, but lower out-of-pocket costs.

- *Silver plans*: Moderate monthly premiums and moderate out-of-pocket costs.

- *Bronze plans*: Lower monthly premiums, but higher out-of-pocket costs.

- *Young Adult plans*: For adults 19 to 26 years old. Young adult plans have low monthly premiums and higher out-of-pocket costs. Most have an annual limit on benefits.

Criticism of Health Care Reform in Massachusetts

Predictably, whether health care reform has succeeded in Massachusetts is a point of great debate. Proponents believe it has done a good job of getting more people insured; opponents say it has raised the cost of health care and created medical shortages.

By far, the biggest criticism of Massachusetts health reform has been its inability to stop rising medical costs. Some critics say it has even increased the cost of care and insurance premiums. In addition, critics say there are now shortages of providers, and thus people have to wait longer to see doctors.

Still, a 2010 report by The Urban Institute and sponsored by the Blue Cross Blue Shield of Massachusetts Foundation concluded that overall, health care reform in the state had met its goals of getting more people insured without eroding insurance coverage offered by employers, stating: "Importantly, the strong system of public coverage in Massachusetts has offset some of the declines in employer-sponsored coverage observed during the economic recession."[1] The report further stated:

> Compared to an analysis for the nation as a whole, health reform in
> Massachusetts appears to have provided more protection against a loss of
> insurance due to the economic downturn for non-elderly adults. Despite the
> importance of public coverage in the state, the majority of Massachusetts
> residents continue to obtain insurance coverage through their employer, with no
> evidence that public coverage has crowded-out employer coverage.

Under health care reform in Massachusetts, insurance coverage of non-elderly adults increased 7.7 percentage points between the fall 2006 and fall 2009, the report said. That means 95.2 percent of working adults are now covered, and the rate of uninsured has dropped more than 60 percent.

Other sources, including the state of Massachusetts, report that the rate of uninsured people has plunged even lower, well below 5 percent. Figure 3-1 presents data from the Massachusetts Division of Health Care Finance and Policy that illustrates the dramatic decline in uninsured state residents after health care reform passed in 2006.

When health care reform was passed in 2006, the Urban Institute study noted that the intention was to get more people covered by insurance. The state legislature decided to make that a higher priority than containing costs. The state is now working on the cost problem, and many people believe national health care reform could help with that, the study said.

There are still problems, the study acknowledged. About 1 in 5 adults reported difficulties finding a doctor who would see them, and many people still had problems paying medical bills.

---

[1] The Urban Institute, "Health Reform in Massachusetts: An Update of Fall 2009" (2010), p.1.

Percentage of Massachusetts Residents Without Health Insurance

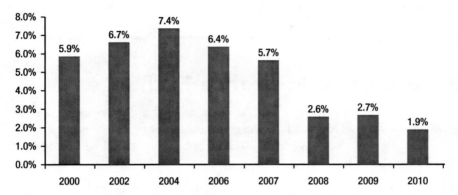

Figure 3-1. The sharp decline in the rate of uninsured Massachusetts residents after health care reform was enacted in 2006. Source: Massachusetts Division of Health Care Finance and Policy.

Nonetheless, support was high for Massachusetts health reform when it passed in 2006, and that support had not wavered by fall 2009, according to polls included in the report. A February 2012 WBUR (Boston's NPR station) poll conducted by the MassINC Polling Group found that 62 percent of Massachusetts residents supported the Massachusetts system and 33 percent opposed it.

MOST FOLLOW INDIVIDUAL MANDATE IN MASSACHUSETTS

Requiring all Americans to purchase insurance is the most unpopular part of the nation's new health care law, but when Massachusetts passed a similar mandate, people generally followed the law.

More than 95 percent of residents in Massachusetts are now purchasing health insurance or having it purchased for them. There has been relatively little short-term purchasing of insurance. If more were occurring, it would indicate that people are only buying insurance when they get ill, thus "gaming the system."

An individual mandate is important when insurers are required to accept all customers, even those with health problems. If people aren't required to have insurance, they can enroll when they are sick and then drop coverage when they are healthy.

That kind of "adverse selection" can be financially disastrous, with health care costs exceeding revenue from premiums. It can lead to financial failure for insurers, or much higher premiums for consumers.

In 2010, the Massachusetts Division of Insurance estimated that part-year insurance purchasing was low, and only increased premiums by about 1 percent—not enough to have much of an impact on the cost of insurance or the financial health of insurers.

Opposition to Insurance Exchanges

After the US Supreme Court ruled in favor of health care reform, several Republican governors decided to delay establishment of an insurance exchange, hoping that the November 2012 elections might lead to the demise of the Affordable Care Act.

But Dr. Bill Frist, a former Republican Senate majority leader and a transplant surgeon, argued in a column for *The Week* magazine that such intransigence was self-defeating. He noted that exchanges foster competition between private insurers and help Americans find the right policies at the right prices.[2]

Frist also noted that states opting out of creating their own exchanges would end up with exchanges created by the federal government. This constitutes a missed opportunity for states to design their own exchanges with their own needs in mind, he said. For example, Utah already has an exchange and wants to coordinate services there with its new exchange. Meanwhile, Vermont eventually intends to transform its exchange into a single-payer system that will provide insurance for all state residents.

"State exchanges ... represent the federalist ideal of states as 'laboratories for democracies,'" Frist wrote.

Individual Mandate Requirements and Penalties

A Harris Interactive/Health Day poll released March 1, 2011, showed that only 22 percent of Americans are comfortable with the idea of forcing most US citizens and legal residents to have minimum medical coverage beginning in 2014.

But a poll by the same organization in February 2010 also showed that 71 percent of Americans understand that nearly everybody needs to be insured to make coverage affordable. They seem to understand that allowing some people to go without insurance would increase costs for everybody else.

---

[2] The Week, "Why Both Parties Should Embrace ObamaCare's State Exchanges," http://theweek.com/bullpen/column/230655/why-both-parties-should-embrace-obamacares-state-exchanges, July 18, 2012.

The Center for American Progress Action Fund points out in a March 23, 2009, analysis that unpaid medical costs from uninsured people are shifted by health care providers to people who are insured. In 2009, this cost-shift amounted to $1,100 per average family premium and $410 per average individual premium, according to the center. Thus, we've got the individual mandate: a kind of necessary evil.

Let's examine a few details of the individual mandate and what happens when people fail to meet it or choose to ignore it.

The mandate requires that, by 2014, most Americans purchase a minimally comprehensive health policy—if they can afford it. That means the insurance must cost less than 8 percent of a person's monthly income. Also, people who fall below the poverty limit or below the threshold for having to file taxes aren't required to purchase insurance.

There are exemptions for other financial hardships and for religious objections, as well as exemptions for Native Americans, incarcerated individuals, undocumented immigrants, citizens living outside the United States, and people who have been uninsured for less than three months. Certificates of exemption will be issued through insurance exchanges.

Most people who get coverage through employers, the new insurance exchanges, the individual market, or any government-sponsored plan will meet the mandate. Insurers will provide the government with the names of policyholders, the number of people insured, the period of insurance, the amount of subsidies, and the type of coverage. Primary policyholders will get a copy of the information.

People who fail to get insurance may pay a fine though the income tax system that will be phased in from 2014 to 2016. The penalty is the greater of a fixed dollar amount per person or a percentage of income above the tax-filing threshold.

▨ **Note** The "filing threshold" is made up of the personal exemption amount, which is doubled for those filing jointly, plus the standard deduction for any given tax year.

The fixed dollar penalty is $95 in 2014, $325 in 2015, and $695 in 2016 and thereafter. For a family, it is capped at 300 percent, or the equivalent of three uninsured people, and the amount is reduced by half for dependents under age 18. The percentage of income above the tax filing threshold that is considered for the fine is 1 percent in 2014, 2 percent in 2015, and 2.5 percent in 2016 and thereafter.

If somebody decides not to buy insurance and not to pay the fine, the IRS will send him or her a notice. If they still don't pay, the IRS can deduct the amount from future refunds. Beyond that, there's not much the government can do. The new health care law says no criminal action or liens can be imposed for failure to pay the fine.

Premiums No Longer Tied to Pre-Existing Medical Conditions

Beginning in 2014, insurers can no longer deny coverage or charge higher premiums to adults with pre-existing medical conditions or poor health. In 2010, a similar law was enacted for children.

Until 2014, the federal government is operating a nationwide network of temporary exchanges that provide insurance coverage to people with pre-existing conditions. After that, people with pre-existing conditions should be able to purchase policies through the permanent network of exchanges or the private market.

When the new rule takes effect, it will essentially mean the end of a process called *medical underwriting*, or evaluating applicants for coverage. Medical underwriting is far more prevalent when insurers sell policies to individuals or small groups. When selling policies to large groups, insurers can rely upon spreading costs more broadly.

A 2009 survey by the Commonwealth Fund reported that 70 percent of adults with health problems found it difficult or impossible to find an affordable plan on the individual market with the coverage they needed, and nearly half were turned down or charged a higher premium because of a pre-existing condition.

Rights to Appeal, Choose Doctor, and Preventive Care

The new health care law is filled with consumer protections, including measures that prohibit insurers from canceling policies or denying coverage to customers who are ill.

The law also forbids rating insurance customers by gender, a practice that has allowed carriers in some states to charge women more than men for identical coverage.

Additionally, the law includes a process that allows policyholders to appeal an insurer's decision to deny a claim. Policyholders must receive detailed information about why a claim is being denied, and how to appeal. There is a process to follow within the insurance company, and another that can be pursued through an independent third party not employed by the insurer.

Also, if a health plan requires the designation of a primary care provider, the policyholder has the right to choose that doctor, as long as the doctor is within the provider network and accepting new patients. The law also allows policyholders to select a pediatrician for a child who is being covered.

And the new health reform law provides direct access to OB/GYNs for women in health plans requiring the designation of primary care providers. That means women can see an OB/GYN without prior authorization or referral.

One of the most extensive changes in health care is a requirement that new policies issued after 2010 cover a long list of preventive care services without any out-pocket costs to consumers. These services are not free; they're being paid through premiums automatically. The following is a partial list of these services:

- Blood pressure, diabetes, and cholesterol tests
- Cancer screenings, including mammograms and colonoscopies
- Flu and pneumonia shots
- Routine vaccines ranging from routine childhood immunizations to periodic tetanus shots for adults, including diseases such as measles, polio, or meningitis
- Counseling from health care providers on things like quitting smoking, losing weight, nutrition, depression, and alcohol abuse
- Counseling, screening, and vaccines for pregnancies
- Regular well-baby and well-child visits

The health law provides for wellness programs by making grants available to small employers for up to five years. In addition, employers will be able to offer rewards to workers who participate in wellness programs. The rewards can include things like premium discounts, waivers of cost-sharing requirements, or special health benefits.

Health Care Reform Brings Changes to Income Tax System

In addition to premium credits, there are a multitude of changes coming for the income tax system. Deductions are being reduced, new taxes are being levied, and health savings accounts are being tightened. The following summarizes the changes (and the year the changes begin):

- Over-the-counter drugs that aren't prescribed can no longer be reimbursed through health savings plans (2011).

- A $2,500 per year (2013) limitation on medical expense contributions to a flexible spending account.

- Increased threshold for itemized deduction for unreimbursed medical expenses from 7.5 percent of adjusted gross income to 10 percent (2013). Increase is waived for people over age 65 for tax years 2013 through 2016.

- Increase in Medicare Part A hospital insurance tax rate on wages by 0.9 percent, from 1.45 to 2.35 percent, on earnings over $200,000 for individuals and $250,000 for couples filing jointly. Also, a 3.8 percent tax on unearned income for higher-income taxpayers (2013).

- A tax on individuals without coverage (2014).

- Excise tax on employer-sponsored health plans with values over $10,200 for individuals and $27,500 for families (2020).

Government Drops Long-Term Care Provision

The government had second thoughts about one provision of the new health care law that was intended to help chronically ill or disabled people stay in their homes rather than go into a nursing home.

The provision would have allowed workers to buy long-term care insurance from the government. Then, if disabled by illness or accident, they could have used the insurance to pay for in-home services or, if necessary, a nursing home.

The problem is that this type of plan would attract people who are already in poor health and likely to use the benefits—remember "adverse selection." And the law requires premiums to be set at a level that would guarantee that the program would be solvent for at least 75 years. Thus, the premiums would be so high that they would discourage healthier people from signing up for the program.

In February 2011, Kathleen Sebelius, Secretary of the US Department of Health and Human Services, told a committee that the program was "totally unsustainable."

She said the government was attempting to redesign the program so it would attract more healthy people and become financially viable. However, in October, the Obama Administration announced that the provision had been dropped because it wasn't workable.

Coming Next

The next chapter deals with provisions of health care reform that affect small and large businesses. There are new requirements for insuring workers and penalties for failure to do so. There are also incentives to help smaller businesses insure their workers.

Business Trends

Tackling Taxes, Mandates, Incentives

When it comes to providing workers with medical insurance benefits, employers face a multitude of big changes and challenges under the new health care law.

There are tax credits for small businesses that *do* offer their workers insurance, and tax penalties for large businesses that *don't*. There are new IRS reporting requirements for small and large businesses.

There are incentives to provide retirees with insurance coverage, and there are complex rules and regulations for businesses that want to keep offering their employees existing insurance plans.

Some provisions of the new law affecting employers have already have been implemented. The following provides a summary of these provisions listed by the year they go into effect:

In 2010, the new health care law

- Started providing tax credits to employers with a maximum of 25 workers and average annual wages of less than $50,000. To qualify, employers must pay 50 percent of premiums. Phase I will run until 2013, and offers a tax credit up to 35 percent—or 25 percent for non-profit organizations—of an employer's cost.

- Created a $5 billion reimbursement program for employers that provide health insurance coverage to early retirees over age 55 who are not eligible for Medicare. This program runs until 2014 or until the money runs out.

In 2011, the new health care law

- Imposed $2.5 billion in annual taxes on the pharmaceutical industry.

- Changed definitions for qualified medical expenses related to flexible spending accounts, health savings accounts, and medical savings accounts.

- Increased distribution penalties from 10 percent to 20 percent for health savings accounts, and from 15 percent to 20 percent for medical savings accounts.

In 2012, the new health care law

- Requires employers to disclose on W-2 forms the cost of each employee's health insurance benefit, although this does not make the benefit taxable.

In 2013, the new health care law

- Increases Medicare tax by 0.9 percent for individuals earning more than $200,000 a year or for families earning more than $250,000 a year. Also for this group, it levies a Medicare Contribution Surtax of 3.8 percent on unearned income.

- Levies a 2.3 percent excise tax on medical device sales, but excludes items such as eyeglasses and hearing aids. Many home medical equipment items such as wheelchairs are also excluded.

- Caps flexible spending account contributions at $2,500.

- Limits to $500,000 the amount insurers can claim as a tax deduction for executive compensation.

- Ends the tax deduction for Medicare Part D subsidy expenses that some employers were paying.

In 2014, the new health care law

- Starts Phase II of tax credits for employers with fewer than 25 workers and average annual wages of less than $50,000. To qualify, employers must pay 50 percent of the premiums for employees. The Phase II tax credit is 50 percent—or 35 percent for non-profit organizations —of an employer's cost if insurance is purchased through an exchange for two years.

- Levies penalties against employers with more than 50 workers, and with at least one worker who purchases insurance through new exchanges and receives a tax credit or subsidy to help pay premiums. For employers that *don't* offer health insurance, the penalty is $2,000 per full-time employee, minus the first 30 employees. For businesses that *do* offer health insurance below government standards, the penalty is the lesser of $2,000 for each employee or $3,000 for each employee who gets tax support.

- Requires employers that do offer workplace coverage to provide a free choice voucher to certain employees—those with incomes less than 400 percent of the federal poverty level and whose share of the premium under the employer-sponsored coverage exceeds 8 percent but is less than 9.8 percent of their income. The free choice vouchers can be used by employees to help pay premiums at one of the new insurance exchanges, which would allow employers to avoid penalties.

- Opens insurance exchanges to small businesses. The exchanges will serve businesses with fewer than 100 employees, although some states may set the cutoff at fewer than 50 employees until 2016. Later, the exchanges may be open to large businesses.

- Permits employers to offer workers rewards of up to 30 percent of the cost of coverage for participating in wellness programs and meeting certain health-related standards.

- Requires employers with more than 200 employees to automatically enroll workers in health insurance plans upon hiring. Maximum waiting period is 90 days, and employees may opt out of coverage.

- Imposes non-deductible, annual $8 billion in taxes proportionately on the health insurance industry.

- Increases estimated tax payment factor by 15.75 percent for corporations with assets over $1 billion.

- Requires employers to report to the IRS information about insurance coverage plans, premiums, and penalties.

In 2018, the new health care law

- Imposes a so-called "Cadillac" insurance plan tax for higher-cost health plans paid by employers. It caps the value of health plans at $10,200 for single coverage or $27,500 for family coverage by levying a 40 percent nondeductible tax on employees for amounts exceeding those caps.

Law Attempts to Give Small Businesses Relief from Big Insurance Costs

Businesses with fewer than 25 workers were targeted for tax relief under the new health law because they face higher insurance costs than large businesses, and they are less likely to provide their workers with insurance.

There are many reasons that insurance is so expensive for small businesses. They often must pay broker fees, and administrative and medical costs can't be spread as broadly over small groups as they can be over large groups. Small businesses can easily pay about 20 percent more for coverage than large businesses.

As a result, fewer small businesses provide health insurance to workers. Only about half of companies with fewer than ten workers offered insurance in 2008. That same year, nearly all firms with more than 100 workers offered some sort of health insurance.

Percentage of All Firms Offering Health Benefits, 1999–2009

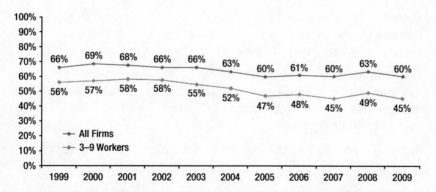

Source: "Employer Sponsored Health Insurance – A Comparison of the Availability and Cost of Coverage for Workers in Small Firms and Large Firms - Snapshot," The Henry J. Kaiser Family Foundation, November 2009

Figure 4-1. A steady decline of employee-sponsored health insurance by all companies. Source: This information was reprinted with permission from the Henry J. Kaiser Family Foundation.

Figure 4-1 shows the decline in companies offering their workers insurance benefits. Figure 4-2 shows that in general, the larger the employer, the more likely they will offer health insurance.

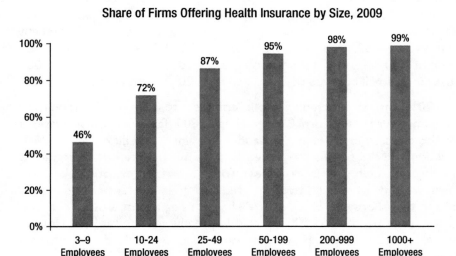

Share of Firms Offering Health Insurance by Size, 2009

Figure 4-2. Smaller businesses are less likely to provide insurance to workers. Health care reform is trying to encourage these businesses to help workers with premiums. Source: This information was reprinted with permission from the Henry J. Kaiser Family Foundation.

Tax Credit for Small Businesses Started in 2010

The new health care law in 2010 initiated the first of many tax incentives it will provide for small businesses that help employees cover the costs of insurance premiums. It is a tax credit for smaller businesses that cover at least half the cost of their workers' insurance.

To be eligible, employers must:

- Cover at least 50 percent of the cost of health care coverage for some workers, based on rates for individuals.

- Have the equivalent of fewer than 25 full-time workers. For example, an employer with fewer than 50 half-time workers might be eligible, according to the IRS.

- Pay average annual wages below $50,000.

The tax credit amounts to 35 percent of a small business's premium costs. The credit is 25 percent for tax-exempt employers. The rate increases to

50 percent (35 percent for tax-exempt employers) on January 1, 2014, but policies must be purchased through exchanges for two years.

The tax credit phases out gradually for firms with average wages between $25,000 and $50,000, and for firms with the equivalent of between 10 and 25 full-time workers. For example, the IRS says a small business that pays $50,000 a year toward workers' health care premiums—and qualifies for a 15 percent credit—will save $7,500 annually from tax year 2010 through 2013 for a total savings of $30,000. The savings would increase from $7,500 to $12,000 annually for a small business that qualified for a 20 percent credit.

In May 2012, the IRS directed for-profit businesses to claim the credit on their income tax returns using Form 8941 and Form 3800. Tax-exempt organizations were also directed to use form 8941 and then claim the credit on Form 990-T. In addition, the IRS has just revamped its page on the Internet dedicated to explaining the credit. It is available through www.irs.gov. Some business owners were delighted to have the credit. "My accountant tells me that, thanks to the Affordable Care Act, we'll be receiving almost a $15,000 health care tax credit on the $90,000 we paid in premiums last year," Jim Houser, who employs 15 people at Hawthorne Auto Clinic in Portland, Oregon, told the *Business Journal of Portland* in a January 28, 2011, article. "That's big money for a small business like mine."

But the small business tax credit has failed to meet expectations of the Obama Administration, which predicted millions of small businesses would benefit from the program. A May 14, 2012, report from the Government Accountability Office found that only about 170,000 small businesses claimed the credit even though up to an estimated 4 million were eligible. One problem was that many very small businesses don't offer health insurance to employees, and the credit wasn't large enough to encourage them to offer it. In addition, many employers just didn't want to spend the time and effort needed to calculate the credit, the Government Accountability Office reported.

COST OF HEALTH INSURANCE CALCULATED BY THE HOUR

Most of us have heard the statistic about employee health insurance benefits adding an average $1,500 to the cost of every Chevrolet. That number was floating around a few years ago when General Motors was in financial trouble.

Indeed, health insurance does add expense to the cost of all products and services. The following facts are from the US Bureau of Labor Statistics (March 2010):

- The average cost for health insurance benefits was $2.08 per hour worked in private industry.

- Employer costs for health insurance benefits were significantly higher for union workers, averaging $4.38 per hour worked, than for nonunion workers, averaging $1.82 per hour.

- In goods-producing industries, health insurance benefit costs were higher, at $2.88 per hour worked, than in service-providing industries, at $1.92 per hour.

- Among the four regions, costs for health insurance benefits were $1.78 per hour in the South, $2.40 per hour in the Northeast, $2.21 per hour in the Midwest, and $2.11 per hour in the West.

The following figure illustrates the breakdown of employer costs per hour worked by industry, occupation, and union status.

Employer costs per hour worked for health insurance, private industry workers, by occupation, union status, and industry, March 2010

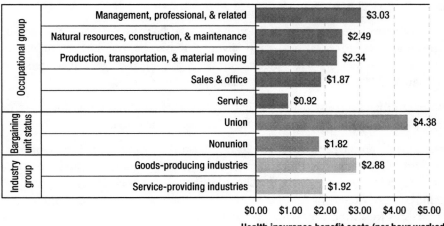

Source: U.S. Bureau of Labor Statistics.

The cost of health insurance per hour in different occupations and groups. Source: US Bureau of Labor Statistics.

Be Careful Counting If You Are Counting on a Tax Credit

There are nuances to the tax credit for small businesses. For instance, the law requires firms to count part-time workers to come up a full-time-equivalency total of no more than 25, but it gets adjusted a tad. So if a firm has 50 workers, as mentioned, it may qualify for the tax credit if the workers are all half-time employees.

The IRS is pretty specific in defining how workers must be counted. Full-time-equivalent employees are counted by taking the total annual hours of a worker's paid service up to a maximum of 2,080 hours. Add all the workers' hours together, and divide that number by 2,080. If it's not a whole number, round to the next *lowest* whole number.

The IRS provides variations in how to make this count, such as equivalencies in days or weeks worked. Go to www.irs.gov and search for "Small Business Health Care Tax Credit: Frequently Asked Questions" for more details.

Qualification for the tax credit is not based upon the number of employees signing up for insurance; it is based upon the total number of employees. So if an employer has 20 full-time-equivalent employees who sign up for insurance, and has another six who don't sign up for insurance, the employer does not qualify for the tax credit because, with a total of 26, it has one too many workers, according to the IRS.

The maximum average wage is calculated by adding up the total amount of money paid to workers, and then dividing it by the number of full-time-equivalent employees. That produces an average annual wage, which must be less than $50,000 for a business to qualify for the tax credit.

Employers must subsidize at least half the cost of premiums for the costs of single (not family) health care coverage for each employee.

Generally, an employer's costs are based upon the amount paid for workers' premiums to an insurer. Medical, dental, and vision plans are included, but there are rules on how costs for these differing plans can be aggregated for the purpose of qualifying for the credit. There are no reductions in the credit or penalties for employers who also receive a health care tax credit or subsidy from states that offer them.

HOW TO COUNT FULL-TIME-EQUIVALENT EMPLOYEES

Here's a simplified IRS example explaining one method of counting full-time equivalent employees for the small business tax credit.

An employer has five workers who are each paid for 2,080 hours, three workers who are each paid for 1,040 hours, and one worker who is paid for 2,300 hours.

Full-time-equivalent employees would be calculated as follows:

- 10,400 hours total for the five workers paid for 2,080 hours each.

- 3,120 hours total for the three workers paid for 1,040 hours each.

- 2,080 hours for the one worker paid for 2,300 hours, since 2,080 hours is the maximum that can be counted for an employee.

So the employer ends up with a total of 15,600 hours, which is divided by 2,080. That comes out to 7.5, which is rounded to the next lowest whole number. That gives the employer seven full-time-equivalent workers.

Costs are capped by the average premium paid in a state's small group market, as determined by the US Department of Health and Human Services (HHS).

And the amount of the credit has a limit. It may not exceed the total of income and Medicare taxes the employer is required to withhold from wages for the year, plus the employer's share of the Medicare tax.

There are a host of IRS rules about what an employer *can't* count as costs paid for premiums. These include, for example, the following:

- The cost of insuring an employer's family members can't be counted, even if they work at the business.

- Generally, the cost of insuring business owners can't be counted.

- Employer contributions to reimbursement plans such as health savings accounts can't be counted.

- Salary reductions in lieu of insurance benefits can't be counted.

- Insurance paid for a leased employee can't be counted.

Grandfathering, or Keeping Your Existing Plan, Requires Complex Calculations

Before going further, let's take a quick look at the concept of "grandfathered" health plans, or attempting to keep an existing insurance plan under health care reform.

■ **Caution** Grandfathering policies will be largely left up to insurers, and many have already decided not to treat any plans this way because of administrative difficulties and costs. Ask your insurer if your plan is being grandfathered.

To keep a grandfathered status, a plan must exist before March 23, 2010. It can't change carriers, substantially change benefits, or increase the coinsurance, deductibles, or out-of-pocket maximums. Some adjustments are allowed for inflation, and grandfathered plans can add new employees and dependents.

There are special rules for plans established under collective bargaining before March 23, 2010. They retain grandfathered status until the agreement expires, and then they face the same requirements as other plans.

Grandfathered plans still have to implement many elements of health care reform, but they are exempt from others. This is discussed in Chapter 3.

The new health care law prohibits carriers from rating premiums based upon the industry or occupation of a small group. But insurers can continue to rate grandfathered plans that way.

The new law prohibits group health plans from providing better benefits to high-paid executives than to other, lower-paid workers. This practice can continue with grandfathered plans if it was already allowed.

Larger Employers Required to Report Insurance Value on W-2 Forms

Beginning for the 2012 tax year, the cost of insurance coverage under an employer-sponsored group plan must be reported by larger employers on W-2 forms typically issued in January 2013. The requirement is optional—for the 2012 tax year only—for employers issuing fewer than 250 W-2 forms.

The reporting requirement does not mean the coverage is taxable. It remains excludable from an employee's income.

The value of health care coverage will be reported on Box 12 of the W-2 form, with Code DD to indentify the amount. There is no reporting required on Form W-3. The amount reported on Form W-2 should include the portion paid by the employer and the employee. Employers are not required to issue a W-2 form solely to report the value of health care coverage of retirees or other employees who normally would not receive a W-2 form.

The value of the following types of coverage must be reported:

- Major medical
- Health FSA value for the plan year in excess of employee's cafeteria plan salary reductions for all qualified benefits
- Hospital indemnity or specified illness (insured or self-funded), paid through salary reduction (pre-tax) or by employer
- Employee Assistance Plan (EAP) providing applicable employer-sponsored health care coverage—if employer charges a COBRA premium
- On-site medical clinics providing applicable employer-sponsored health care coverage—if employer charges a COBRA premium
- Wellness programs providing applicable employer-sponsored health care coverage—if the employer charges a COBRA premium
- Domestic partner coverage included in gross income

Optional items that may be reported include dental and vision plans, Health Reimbursement Arrangement (HRA) contributions, multi-employer plans, self-funded plans not subject to COBRA, and, if employers does not charge a COBRA premium, EAP coverage, on-site medical clinics and wellness programs.

The IRS also has a YouTube video on "W-2 Health Insurance Reporting." You can search on the Internet for "IR-2011-31".

Requirement for Coverage and Penalties for Not Doing So

Starting on January 1, 2014, excise tax penalties begin for larger employers that either don't provide insurance or do provide insurance at subpar levels. It is commonly called an employer "pay or play" requirement.

Small businesses with fewer than 50 employees are exempt, and the penalties are expected to have a minimal impact on large or mid-sized employers that already offer reasonably good health insurance benefits to workers.

HOW TO COUNT EMPLOYEES FOR TAX PENALTIES

There has been much attention focused on regulations expected from the government in 2012 that will set the standard for a full-time employee when it comes to calculating penalties for failure to provide coverage.

The Obama Administration proposed setting the standard at an average of 30 hours a week with a three-month look back period beginning in 2014. The Retail Industry Leaders Association and other groups were seeking a transition period until 2016 that would allow employers to work toward complying with the law without being penalized.

Also, groups also have been concerned about employees shifting or "churning" back and forth between employer coverage and exchange coverage, depending on their status. Thus, more flexibility is being sought in determining full-time status, particularly for businesses that employ seasonal workers or workers with highly variable hours.

There is no penalty for any employer as long as none of their employees goes to a health exchange, purchases insurance, and receives a tax credit or subsidy to help pay premiums.

But large employers that don't offer insurance will have to pay an annual tax penalty of $2,000 per employee, with the penalty waived for the first 30 employees.

Penalties get a little more complicated when an employer offers insurance that falls short of government guidelines for full coverage, or fails to pass an "affordability test." That means the insurance may fall short of minimum standards for what it covers, or an employee's portion of the premium payment exceeds 9.5 percent of household income. Inadequate health insurance coverage enables a worker to go to an exchange, and if qualified, get a tax credit or subsidy—which triggers a $3,000 penalty against the employer.

The US Department of the Treasury in 2011 said this "affordability test" would apply only to single coverage. However, this raised concerns that a worker could end up with sufficient coverage, but the worker's family could fall between the cracks—and not be eligible for either coverage through an employer or an exchange. In 2012, the Treasury Department said it would reconsider the issue, and may decide the affordability test should also apply to family coverage.

There is a way to work around the penalties with certain employees. In 2014, employers that offer workplace coverage must provide free-choice vouchers to employees with incomes less than 400 percent of the federal poverty level, and whose share of the premium exceeds 8 percent but is less than 9.8 percent of income.

The vouchers can be used by employees to help pay premiums at one of the new insurance exchanges, and this allows employers to avoid penalties—but only if the workers use vouchers instead of accepting tax credits and subsidies.

For employers that offer subpar health insurance, penalties are prorated on a monthly basis and amount to $3,000 multiplied by the number of employees who get tax credits or subsidies through exchanges. The penalty cannot exceed the amount a business would pay if it didn't offer insurance at all— $2,000 multiplied by the number of employees.

EMPLOYER-SPONSORED INSURANCE ON DOWNHILL SLIDE

For decades, a majority of Americans have been insured through their employers. But the number of Americans who are insured this way is steadily dropping.

As policy prices skyrocketed over the past decade, the number of employer-sponsored insurance plans decreased, and the number of workers covered by them declined. That has created a problem, since employer-sponsored health insurance has been the most affordable coverage for most Americans.

And conditions worsened during the recession, with firms cutting their insurance benefits and shifting more costs to employees, as shown in the following figure.

Among Firms Offering Health Benefits, Percentage of Firms That Report They Made the Following Changes as a Result of the Economic Downturn, by Firm Size, 2010

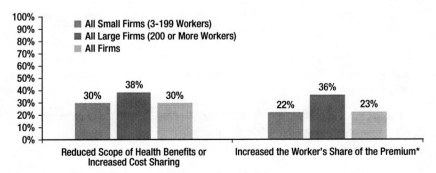

*Estimate is statistically different between all Small Firms and Large Firms within the category (p<.05)
Source: Kaiser Slides, The Henry J. Kaiser Family Foundation and HRET, September 2010

Many employers reduced health benefits for workers during the recession. Source: This information was reprinted with permission from the Henry J. Kaiser Family Foundation.

The decline of employer-sponsored plans is one reason health care reform was passed.

Oddly, the new law may accelerate the decline of employer-sponsored health insurance, some experts believe. There are many reasons to think this, including

- In 2014, insurance exchanges will come online and offer affordable alternatives to employer-sponsored health insurance.

- Also in 2014, Medicaid will expand eligibility and provide free insurance to millions of low-income workers, some of whom would otherwise be covered by workplace insurance.

- Then, in 2018, a 40 percent excise tax will be levied against high-end or "Cadillac" employer-sponsored insurance plans, essentially making those policies less affordable.

Health care reform does provide incentives for smaller businesses to offer insurance to workers, but those incentives gradually expire. The new law also penalizes employers for not providing insurance to workers, but the penalties are less than the cost of coverage.

And in a twist on the new law, research from the Center for Studying Health System Change finds that some small business are expressing a growing interest in self-insuring their employees. That would reduce regulations on coverage and participation in insurance exchanges.

Meanwhile, some experts see the move away from employer-sponsored insurance as a positive trend. It will allow workers more mobility, put them in a better position to make decisions about insurance, and make them aware of the real cost of health care. It will also lower costs for employers.

Other experts are concerned because employer-sponsored plans have done a good job of keeping insurance costs spread thin by creating large pools of policyholders. Administrative costs have been fairly low, too.

And perhaps the most important contribution to health care by American businesses has been the huge amount of money that companies have spent in subsidizing insurance premium for workers.

Unfortunately, as insurance has become more expensive, workers on average have ended up with larger increases in premium costs than employers, as illustrated in the following figure.

Average Annual Health Insurance Premiums and Worker Contributions
for Family Coverage, 2005-2010

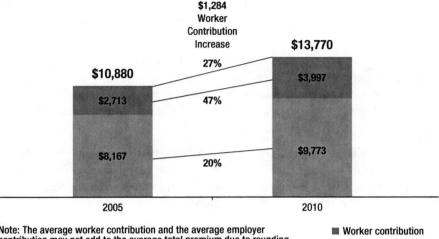

$1,284
Worker
Contribution
Increase

Note: The average worker contribution and the average employer
contribution may not add to the average total premium due to rounding.

Source: Kaiser Slides, The Henry J. Kaiser Family Foundation and HRET,
September 2010

■ Worker contribution
■ Employer Contribution

The rising cost of insurance premiums has hit employers and employees, but it's hit employees hardest. Source: This information was reprinted with permission from the Henry J. Kaiser Family Foundation.

Small Businesses May Shop at Insurance Exchanges

Beginning in 2014, insurance exchanges will open to small employers through the Small Business Options Program, or SHOP.

Most exchanges are expected to provide services to businesses with fewer than 100 employees, but states have the option of limiting the access to only businesses with fewer than 50 employees until 2016. States also have the option of opening exchanges to businesses with more than 100 employees in 2017.

SHOP is expected to allow employers to shop for qualified coverage and more easily compare prices and benefits. The program is also aimed at self-employed Americans, who have been largely limited to shopping in the individual insurance market. The program will offer tax credits to the self-employed of $1,800 for individual coverage and $3,600 for family coverage.

SHOP exchanges will form a nationwide purchasing pool that will offer plans in every state. However, plans will still have to meet regulations for the state in which they are issued. The government hopes these pools will reduce administrative costs and provide a more efficient way for insurers to market health plans.

Reforms in how insurers rate plans should make premiums more stable and affordable. Beginning in 2012, health status ratings will no longer be permitted in small group markets, which essentially serve small businesses. That should protect small groups from large premium increases when somebody in a group experiences an expensive illness.

Over time, SHOP exchanges are expected to reduce variations in premium rates based upon age, and that should help make plans more affordable for older Americans who are self-employed. However, there will be a surcharge placed on people who wait to enroll in plans until they are older and sicker.

Devil May Be in the Details for SHOP Insurance Plans

Although details have not yet been worked out for SHOP, some early planning has revealed a difference of opinion about how much choice the program should give small businesses and how much choice it should give workers.

During a January 2011 Congress on Health Insurance Reform, there was much debate about whether the exchanges could be set up in a way that workers could make choices about policies without forcing small business into the burdensome task of making individual payments each month to a multitude of plans. Or, would business just pick a few plans and give their workers limited choices?

Also, questions were raised about whether SHOP exchanges would operate through a network of exchanges already being established by states to serve individuals, or if they would operate as separate exchanges.

Note The US Department of Health and Human Services on July 11, 2011, issued final regulations on how states should structure SHOP exchanges. States will have many options on how these exchanges are designed, but SHOP exchanges should help employers find qualified health plans, get information on price and benefits, help enroll employees and consolidate billing.

Early Retiree Reinsurance Program Stops Accepting Applicants

More than 2,000 insurance plans were quickly accepted in 2010 into the Early Retiree Reinsurance Program, an initiative started under health care reform to encourage businesses to offer coverage to early retirees. In May 2011, officials stopped accepting applications.

The program helps employers pay insurance costs for early retirees beginning at age 55 and ending at age 65 when all Americans become eligible for Medicare. The program runs until 2014 when exchanges come online to fill the gap between early retirement and Medicare.

Faced with the skyrocketing cost of insurance premiums, employers have been discontinuing early retiree health benefits, as shown in Figure 4-3.

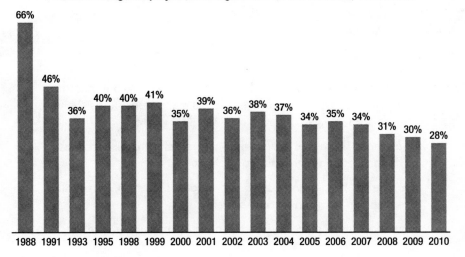

Percent of Large Employers Offering Retiree Health Benefits, 1988–2010

Notes: Large firms include firms with 200 or more workers. Data not available for all years between 1988 and 1998 because the survey was not conducted each year during that period.

Source: Kaiser Slides, The Henry J. Kaiser Family Foundation and HRET, November 2010

Figure 4-3. The decline in employers with more than 200 workers who offer early retirees a health insurance benefit to fill a coverage gap until Medicare starts at age 65. Source: This information was reprinted with permission from the Henry J. Kaiser Family Foundation.

Without this benefit, early retirees are often forced to buy insurance on the private individual market, which can be expensive. Insurers routinely charge retirees from 55 to 64 years of age much higher premiums for far less coverage than younger people. Also, insurers may exclude pre-existing conditions for early retirees, or they may not offer them coverage at all.

The new program is providing $5 billion to employers and unions to help maintain coverage for early retirees. In September 2010, applicants started submitting claims dated back to June 1, 2010. As of May 5, 2011, the HHS no longer accepted applications into the program because of diminishing funding.

Employers and unions accepted into the program are reimbursed for medical claims for early retirees and their spouses, surviving spouses, and dependents.

In the early months of the program, nearly 3,000 applications were approved and represented in nearly every sector of the economy, with 32 percent coming from businesses, 26 percent from state and local governments, 22 percent from unions, 14 percent from educational institutions, and 5 percent from not-for-profit organizations.

HHS Secretary Kathleen Sebelius said her agency's Office of Consumer Information and Insurance Oversight had received applications from more than half of the *Fortune* 500 companies, all major unions, and government agencies in all states.

To be eligible, employers or unions were required to

- Maintain either directly or through an insurer, a group health plan that provides coverage to early retirees and their immediate families.

- Implement programs to provide care efficiently to enrollees with chronic and high-cost conditions.

- Be able to document claims for medical, surgical, hospital, prescription drug, and other benefits.

- Have policies in place to detect and reduce fraud, waste, and abuse.

The program generally applied Medicare standards in determining whether a benefit was eligible for reimbursement. The program pays 80 percent of the actual health cost paid by or on behalf of an individual. Reimbursement starts after a retiree hits $15,000 in medical costs, and ends when costs exceed $90,000.

Money that is reimbursed by the government must be used to reduce cost of benefits for the company or union, or lower premiums and out-of-pocket costs for plan participants. The money may not be used for general revenue.

In its first six months, the program paid out more than $500 million in reimbursements for health services provided to 60,859 people.

Exchanges Expected to Provide Relief to Early Retirees

The Early Retiree Reinsurance Program ends when the initial $5 billion is spent, or on December 31, 2013, the day before state-based insurance exchanges are supposed to open.

Authorities say these exchanges will provide insurance relief to early retirees by offering guaranteed coverage and clear choices between several plans.

This will also lift from business the burden of finding insurance plans for a large group of people with widely diverse needs and often very expensive conditions.

In addition, some authorities believe that early retirees could evolve into "super consumers" when shopping at insurance exchanges. Studies with Medicare participants have shown that older people with a limited budget often become extremely savvy insurance shoppers.

New Law Creates Incentives for Employee Wellness Programs

Studies have shown that wellness programs can save employers $3 for every $1 spent. So it's not surprising that these programs, which encourage healthy lifestyles and require workers to meet certain medical standards, have been growing for years. A poll released in November 2011 by the human resources consulting firm Mercer found that 87 percent of large employers with more than 500 employees were planning to add or strengthen wellness programs or policies.

The new health care law encourages further growth of these programs by

- Awarding grants for up to five years to small employers that establish wellness programs.
- Providing technical assistance and other resources to evaluate employer-based wellness programs.
- Conducting a national worksite health policies and programs survey to assess employer-based health policies and programs.

- Permitting employers to offer increased employee rewards—in the form of premium discounts, waivers of cost-sharing requirements, or benefits that would otherwise not be provided.

- Establish a ten-state pilot program by July 2014 to permit study of a widely instituted wellness program. If effective, the program would be expanded in 2017.

While offering a wellness program may sound simple, it's actually a fairly complicated process. Programs must meet a host of regulations ensuring health privacy and workplace fairness.

For instance, under the new health care law employers can increase rewards up to 30 to 50 percent of the cost of insurance coverage for employees who participate in a wellness program and meet certain health-related standards. Previously, the limit was 20 percent.

But employers must offer an alternative standard for some people who have medical conditions that make is difficult to meet the program's primary standards.

Warning Some human resource managers are concerned that the cost of wellness programs might be included in the overall worth of an insurance program by the government, and trigger the 2018 excise tax on "Cadillac" insurance plans. This, along with other details about Cadillac insurance plans, will likely need to be clarified by the IRS.

HIPAA RULES CLARIFIED FOR WELLNESS PROGRAMS

Federal agencies in 2006 issued rules and regulations meant to clarify rules for wellness programs under the Health Insurance Portability and Accountability Act, better known as HIPAA.

Regulators said the following wellness programs are acceptable:

- A program that pays for fitness center memberships.

- A diagnostic testing program providing rewards for participation, but not basing any part of the reward on outcomes.

- A program that encourages preventive care through waiver of a co-payment or deductible requirements in a group insurance plan.

- A program that reimburses employees for the cost of smoking cessation programs. Whether or not the employee quits smoking cannot be a factor in payment.

- A program that rewards employees for attending monthly health education seminars.

Rules are a little different for wellness programs that base rewards on health factors. They must

- Be reasonably designed to promote health or prevent disease.

- Give eligible individuals an annual opportunity to qualify for rewards.

- Be available to everybody. This means the program must provide a "reasonable alternative standard" for people with medical conditions that make it unreasonably difficult for them to meet the program's primary standards.

In addition to meeting HIPAA regulations, wellness programs must follow rules set by the Genetic Information Non-Discrimination Act, which is intended to protect people against workplace discrimination based upon genetic pre-disposition for some medical conditions.

That means there are severe limits on employers gathering family medical histories of employees, even if the information is being used for a wellness program.

Coming Next

In many ways, health care reforms lands at the feet of the health insurance industry. The new law was passed largely because people believed, rightly or wrongly, that insurers were abusing the health care system by running up excessive profits, unfairly canceling policies, and cutting or denying benefits.

Now, insurers face a myriad of new rules and regulations that limit earnings, increase oversight, and set standards for coverage. We'll look at some of those in the next chapter.

Insurance Shift

Law Changes Market Rules, Regulations

Health care reform makes drastic changes to the insurance industry's marketplace. Among other things, it changes the way insurance is sold, it sets requirements for what policies must cover, it mandates that everybody be offered coverage, and it attempts to cap administrative costs, profits, and overhead. In short, it closes some opportunities and opens others, particularly with the influx of an estimated 16 million new customers.

Before health care reform, insurers had plenty of leeway. They generally based premium prices on actuarial principles, claims experience, or the health condition of customers. State and federal regulations allowed them to design products pretty much as they pleased. They could limit what some policies covered, even excluding conditions such as maternity care. They could set co-pays and deductibles as competition dictated, and they were allowed to place annual and lifetime limits on policies. They decided whom to cover and whom not to cover.

That all changes under the new health care law, and it would be impossible to quickly explain in detail all the new rules. Insurers and regulators are now struggling to understand the complex medical and financial implications of the Patient Protection and Affordable Care Act of 2010.

But there are aspects of the law's impact on insurers that are worth examining, including provisions that require them to do the following:

- Spend a certain percentage of premiums on medical care for policyholders. In the industry, it's called a medical loss ratio, and it has resulted in more than $1 billion in premium rebates to policyholders.

- Offer coverage to all customers, regardless of pre-existing medical conditions or age. The new law also prohibits the practice of rescission, or using petty reasons for canceling policies after customers get sick.

- Use community ratings—or charge all policyholders the same, regardless of gender, age, or medical condition—with some important adjustments.

- Include minimal coverage and preventive care in all policies.

- Standardize policies so that customers can make apple-to-apple comparisons when shopping in the new insurance exchanges.

In addition to new requirements for insurers, the new law has provisions that encourage the creation of cooperatives, or insurance companies owned by their customers. We'll also take a quick look at the movement toward accountable care organizations, which operate in a manner similar to some existing cooperatives.

Insurers' Medical Loss Ratio Creates Rebates for Policyholders

In the summer of 2012, about 12.8 million health insurance policyholders nationwide were set to receive $1.1 billion in rebates from insurers who failed to meet a metric called the *medical loss ratio*. The average rebate was $151 per household, and the money was coming as a check in the mail, a reduction of future premiums, or a lump-sum reimbursement to an account from which premiums are paid.

The rebates were the product of a new standard set by health care reform. The medical loss ratio shows the percentage of total premium payments that an insurer spends on medical care for policyholders. The remaining percentage of money from premiums goes to things such as administration, profits, marketing, and other overhead costs.

Health care reform requires that a relatively high percentage of premium dollars be spent on actual health care—85 percent for large groups and 80 percent for smaller groups. Under the new law, insurers failing to meet the standard must issue rebates to customers.

Enacting standards for the medical loss ratio is intended to control profits and bring down overhead, including administrative costs, which are the highest in the developed world, as shown in Figure 5-1.

High U.S. Insurance Overhead: Insurance-Related Administrative Costs

- Fragmented payers + complexity = high transaction costs and overhead costs
  - McKinsey estimates adds $90 billion per year*
- Insurance and providers
  - Variation in benefits; lack of coherence in payment
  - Time and people expense for doctors/hospitals

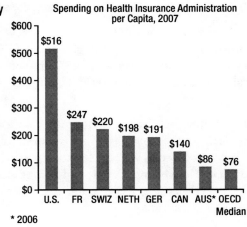

Spending on Health Insurance Administration per Capita, 2007

$600 — $516
$500 — $247
$400 — $220
$300 — $198 $191
$200 — $140
$100 — $86 $76
$0 —

U.S. FR SWIZ NETH GER CAN AUS* OECD Median

* 2006

Figure 5-1. Median administrative costs for private health insurance in the United States have climbed to about $500 per person, more than double those of other developed countries. Source: Commonwealth Fund, with data from the OECD, and "Accounting for the Cost of US Health Care: A New Look at Why Americans Spend More" (McKinsey Global Institute, December 2008).

At first, determining what went into a medical loss ratio was controversial and complicated. At the government's direction, the National Association of Insurance Commissioners attempted to define the medical loss ratio, and proposed a massive new form that would spell out exactly what could be counted as medical costs.

The US Department of Health and Human Services (HHS) issued its final rule on medical loss ratio requirements in December 2011. Among many other details, the 20-page rule includes provisions on special treatment of the medical loss ratio for "mini-med" plans and clarifies the distribution of rebates by insurers in group markets. The rule slowly adjusts the medical loss ratio for mini-med plans, which aren't expected to be allowed after exchanges open in 2014. Since rebates would be taxable, the final rule states that they may be paid to customers in the form of lower premiums or other ways that are not taxable.

The final rule also caused a stir among insurance agents and brokers. They had been lobbying to have fees paid to them exempted from administrative costs and counted as medical care costs. Federal officials decided that these fees should be counted as administrative costs.

The final forms for submitting medical loss ratio reports have been trimmed from original proposals, but they are still fairly complicated. These forms are available at http://ccio.cms.gov/resources/other.

People in the insurance industry say the new medical loss ratio standard is arbitrary and sets operating margins too low for many companies. Even the National Association of Insurance Commissioners in May 2010 noted that medical loss ratios for insurers generally range between 55 percent and 65 percent.

So the government is issuing waivers if it appears that an insurer may leave a market because of inability to meet the new standard. As of January 2012, the government had issued waivers for six states: Georgia, Iowa, Kentucky, Maine, Nevada, and New Hampshire. It had turned down applications for waivers in eight states: Delaware, Florida, Indiana, Kansas, Louisiana, Michigan, North Dakota, and Oklahoma.

Guaranteed Coverage for Everybody, Despite Everything

One of biggest changes to the insurance industry has been the new requirement that, in 2014, coverage must be offered to virtually all customers, regardless of age or infirmity. Already, insurers have been stopped from canceling policies for insignificant reasons or inadvertent errors. In addition, companies will no longer be able to cap coverage at a certain dollar level, like $1 million.

In short, insurers are going to be providing more coverage to customers who run up expensive medical costs.

That is a turnabout. One big reason for enacting health care reform was to end an insurance industry practice called *rescission*—reviewing policies after a policyholder gets sick, and then retroactively canceling coverage over relatively minor mistakes found on old applications. The HHS issued an interim final rule on rescission on September 23, 2010. The rule stated that a health plan could no longer retroactively rescind coverage, except in cases of fraud or misrepresentation of fact by the policyholder. However, it does allow prospective cancellation of coverage, along with prospective or retroactive cancellation of coverage, if a policyholder fails to pay premiums.

While this issue seems simple, it's complicated because the administration of insurance is complicated. The following is an example cited in the interim final rule:

Facts: An employer sponsors a group health plan that provides coverage for employees who work at least 30 hours a week per employee. Individual B has coverage under the plan as a full-time employee. The employer reassigns B to a part-time position. Under terms of the plan, B is no longer eligible for coverage. The plan mistakenly continues to provide health coverage, collecting premiums from B and paying claims submitted by B. After a routine audit, the plan discovers that B no longer works at least 30 hours per week. The plan rescinds B's coverage effective as of the date that B changed from a full-time employee to a part-time employee.

Conclusion: The plan cannot rescind B's coverage because there was no fraud or an intentional misrepresentation of material fact. The plan may cancel coverage for B prospectively, subject to otherwise applicable federal and state laws.

Cutting back on rescission and forcing insurers to accept customers who are very ill will have a big financial impact. For instance, a congressional investigation in 2009 found that three insurers—WellPoint Inc., United HealthGroup, and Assurant Inc.—avoided paying $300 million in medical claims over five years by canceling the policies of about 20,000 people.

Consider the following facts from the HHS, which show that relatively few policyholders account for a large percentage of an insurance company's medical costs:

- Five percent of the population accounts for almost half of total health care expenses.

- The 15 most expensive health conditions account for 44 percent of total health care expenses.

- About half the US population spends virtually nothing on health care, and accounts for only about 3 percent of all medical expenses.

Of course, these are reasons why proponents of health care reform included a mandate requiring virtually all Americans to have insurance. It was the only way costs could be spread thin enough for insurers to survive the onslaught of medical expenses. So in addition to having to accept ill and expensive applicants, the government estimates that health care reform will bring 16 million new customers for private insurers.

HOW THE GOVERNMENT ADDS UP HEALTH CARE REFORM

The Congressional Budget Office estimates that the new health care law will lead to 32 million more Americans obtaining insurance coverage after gains and losses are counted. The following describes how gains and losses break down between 2010 and 2020:

- Add 24 million people who will purchase insurance through the new network of state-based exchanges.

- Add 16 million people who will gain coverage through Medicaid or its related Children's Health Insurance Program (CHIP). (This may change because the Supreme Court ruling allowed states to opt out of the expansion of Medicaid.)

- Subtract 5 million people who will drop their private insurance and shift coverage to exchanges or Medicaid.

- Subtract 3 million people who will stop taking insurance through employers and shift coverage to exchanges or Medicaid.

That comes to 40 million in additions and 8 million in subtractions, for a total gain of 32 million newly insured Americans. Medicaid will get 16 million new beneficiaries, and insurers will get 16 million new customers.

New Law Requires Insurers to Limit Variations in Rates

In addition to requiring insurers to offer coverage to virtually all customers, in 2014 the new health care law also requires that insurers limit the variations in rates it charges customers in the individual and small group market.

It's called community rating, or modified community underwriting, and it refers to a kind of leveling of premium prices among all policyholders in a group. The rule will affect fully insured groups of under 100 policyholders. Large groups don't have as much of a problem with rate variations because medical costs can be spread thinner over a greater number of people.

In the past, insurers often based small group rates on claims experience and other risk factors. Under the new rules, insurers can no longer rate health plans by group demographics or experience with claims. Also, they must accept all applicants regardless of pre-existing health conditions, age, gender, or occupation.

The new law will allow ratings based only on age, family composition, geographical area, and tobacco use. The new law sets the following two limits:

- Insurers will be allowed to charge a tobacco user a premium 1.5 times higher than the premium for a person who doesn't use tobacco.

- A plan's oldest subscriber can be charged no more than three times as much as a plan's youngest subscriber.

States may set limits for family composition and geographic areas.

Critics of community rating say it unfairly makes health insurance rates more expensive for large groups of young and healthy people, and less expensive for small groups of older and less healthy people.

Proponents of community rating say it does precisely what insurance is intended to do—lower costs for somebody who gets sick by shifting it to a large group of people who are well.

In an effort to make community rating fair and efficient, the new law requires states to create systems for making extra payments to insurers who end up with too many ill and expensive customers. This is called *risk adjustment*. For instance, under risk adjustment, money could be taken from an insurer who has many healthy and inexpensive policyholders and shift it to an insurer who has ended up with many sick and expensive customers.

On March 23, 2012, the HHS published a final rule on risk adjustment. The federal government will operate risk-adjustment programs for states that don't want to do it themselves. Through these programs, $10 billion will be collected from insurers in 2014, $6 billion in 2015, and $4 billion in 2016. The government will set rates for contributions.

Medicare already uses risk adjustment in its managed care and prescription drug plan programs.

New Law Sets Minimum Coverage, Preventive Care Coverage

The new health care law sets minimum standards for coverage, and provides a long list of preventive care procedures and services that must be included in policies. Policies sold in exchanges must meet standards that allow them to be easily compared to each other.

Beginning in 2014, health insurance plans purchased at exchanges must include ten categories of "essential health benefits." They are ambulatory patient services; emergency services; hospitalization; maternity and newborn care; mental health and substance use disorder services, including behavioral health treatment; prescription drugs; rehabilitative and habilitative services and devices; laboratory services; preventive and wellness services; chronic disease management; and pediatric services, including oral and vision care.

To meet requirements for the individual mandate, insurance plans purchased outside the exchange system must include "minimum essential coverage," which is only slightly different from "essential health benefits." For a plan to meet "minimum essential coverage," it must

- Provide essential health benefits.

- Limit cost sharing—such as deductibles, co-insurance, and co-payments—for essential health benefits.

- Provide the equivalent of coverage offered through plans at an exchange.

In addition, insurance plans created after March 23, 2010, must provide a defined list of preventive care services and procedures with no out-of-pocket cost to policyholders. What follows are lists of preventive care services, in alphabetical order, included in health care reform for adults, women, and children. For the services to be considered preventive, they must not be delivered as part of care provided after a diagnosis, and for health plans with networks, they must be delivered within the network.

For adults:

- Abdominal aortic aneurysm one-time screening for men of specified ages who have ever smoked

- Alcohol misuse screening and counseling

- Aspirin use for men and women of certain ages

- Blood pressure screening

- Cholesterol screening for adults of certain ages or at higher risk for cardiovascular disease

- Colorectal cancer screening for adults over age 50

- Depression screening

- Type 2 diabetes screening for adults with high blood pressure

- Diet counseling for adults at higher risk for chronic disease

- HIV screening for all adults at higher risk of contracting AIDS

- Immunizations (schedules and qualifications vary): hepatitis A; hepatitis B; herpes zoster; human papillomavirus; influenza; measles, mumps, rubella; meningococcal; pneumococcal; tetanus, diphtheria, pertussis; and varicella

- Obesity screening and counseling

- Sexually transmitted infection prevention counseling for adults at higher risk contracting one of these diseases

- Tobacco use screening for all adults and cessation interventions for tobacco users

- Syphilis screening for all adults at higher risk of contracting this sexually transmitted disease

For women, including those pregnant:

- Anemia screening for pregnant women

- Bacteriuria urinary tract or other infection screening for pregnant women

- BRCA genetic counseling for women at higher risk for breast cancer

- Breast cancer counseling for women who could benefit from drug therapy to prevent the disease

- Breast feeding support

- Cervical cancer screening for sexually active women

- Chlamydia infection screening for younger women and other women at higher risk for this sexually transmitted disease

- Folic acid supplements for women who may become pregnant

- Gonorrhea screening for women at higher risk for contracting this sexually transmitted disease

- Hepatitis B screening for pregnant women at their first prenatal visit

- Mammography screenings every one to two years for women over age 40

- Osteoporosis screening for women over age 60 depending on risk factors

- Rh incompatibility screening for all pregnant women and follow-up testing for women at higher risk for this condition
- Tobacco use screening and interventions for all women, and expanded counseling for pregnant tobacco users
- Syphilis screening for all pregnant women or other women at increased risk for this sexually transmitted disease

For children:

- Alcohol and drug-use assessments for adolescents
- Autism screening for children at ages 18 months and 24 months
- Behavioral assessments
- Cervical dysplasia screening for sexually active girls
- Congenital hypothyroidism screening for newborns
- Developmental screening for children under age 3, and surveillance throughout childhood
- Dyslipidemia screening for children at higher risk of lipid disorders
- Fluoride supplements for children without fluoride in their water source
- Gonorrhea preventive medication for the eyes of all newborns
- Hearing screening for all newborns
- Height, weight, and body mass index measurements
- Hematocrit or hemoglobin screening
- HIV screening for adolescents at higher risk of contracting AIDS
- Immunization for children from birth to age 18 (doses, ages, and conditions vary): diphtheria, tetanus, pertussis; haemophilus influenza Type B; hepatitis A; hepatitis B; human papillomavirus; inactivated poliovirus; influenza; measles, mumps, rubella; meningococcal; pneumococcal; rotavirus; and varicella
- Iron supplements for children ages 6 to 12 months at risk for anemia

- Lead screening for children at risk of exposure

- Medical history throughout development

- Obesity screening and counseling

- Oral health risk assessment for young children

- Phenylketonuria (PKU) screening for this genetic disorder in newborns

- Sexually transmitted infection prevention counseling for adolescents at higher risk of contracting these diseases

- Sickle cell screening for newborns

- Tuberculosis testing for children at higher risk of contracting this disease

- Vision screening

Addition of Birth Control to Preventive Care Creates Controversy

In August 2011, the US Department of Health and Human Services issued an interim final rule expanding the list of preventive care services that insurers must offer to women on policies that are new or renewing after August 1, 2012. The most controversial addition was a requirement that most insurers add contraceptive services without co-pay for women policyholders. It exempted some religious organizations but not all, particularly those with missions not entirely religious, such as hospitals.

Religious groups objected. Federal officials attempted to craft a compromise that would have had insurance companies provide birth control services, and allow all religious institutions to opt out, essentially funneling premiums payments and coverage through insurers. It extended the deadline for coverage to August 1, 2013. Some leaders in the Catholic Church still felt the rule implied tacit approval on the Church's part to provide birth control services. To complicate things further, some religious institutions self-insure, which means they would not have an insurance company to act as a conduit for providing birth control services.

On May 21, 2012, forty-three leading Catholic institutions in eight states filed a lawsuit claiming that the rule infringed upon religious liberty and was unconstitutional. Although they had been working on a compromise with the federal government, there was rising concern among Catholic institutions about the approaching of August 1, 2013, deadline to have the new preventive services for women in place. So the lawsuit was filed.

On one hand, the Catholic Church is saying it shouldn't be required to do something that violates tenets of its faith. On the other hand, federal health officials are saying that all women should have a right to birth control without co-pays as part of a package of preventive care services, and many states already require such coverage.

Other preventive services added for women in August 2011 included yearly wellness visits, breastfeeding equipment, and screening for gestational diabetes, domestic abuse, HPV, and HIV.

Health Care Reform Cracks the Door for Insurance Co-Ops

One part of the health care reform package that is seldom discussed has to do with the creation of insurance cooperatives, or as the law calls them, Consumer-Owned and -Oriented Plans (CO-OP).

Under the new law, about $6 billion in federal funds would be spent to create and support these consumer-owned-and-operated providers of health insurance. They could operate in individual and small-group markets.

There are already some health insurance cooperatives in existence. Two of the largest are Group Health in Seattle and HealthPartners in Minneapolis. Over the years, many health insurance cooperatives have failed because of competition, lack of resources, and disagreements between co-op boards and health care providers.

Proponents of health insurance cooperatives say these non-profit organizations can serve members better because their focus is on providing insurance, not making money. Cooperatives can provide people with reduced costs and good coverage, and compete with private insurers. Under health care reform, consumers could form a co-op and negotiate for services directly with providers.

Cooperatives would be self-governed by an elected board of members, but would have to operate as part of the national network of insurance exchanges created under health care reform.

Members would determine premiums, benefits, deductibles, and co-pays. Surpluses would be returned to members as reduced premiums and better benefits. Health insurance cooperatives would be exempt from federal taxes.

An HHS committee started working on guidelines for cooperatives in June 2010, and grants and loans are supposed to be awarded by July 1, 2013.

Insurance industry insiders are skeptical of this aspect of health care reform because creating an insurance company is filled with financial, legal, and medical complexities. And cooperatives are not allowed to be affiliated with insurance companies, which cuts off access to that expertise.

By April 2012, the government had approved ten new co-ops that serve New York, New Jersey, Oregon, Montana, South Carolina, Iowa, New Mexico, Wisconsin, and Maine. Government officials hope to approve enough co-ops to serve all states. Co-op insurance plans will be available through exchanges or in the private market.

GROUP HEALTH—MEDICAL CARE WITH ACCOUNTABILITY

Group Health, based in Seattle, is an insurance cooperative that has been around since 1947. It covers about 600,000 members in Washington state and northern Idaho.

It coordinates most of its care through a network of facilities it owns and operates. That includes twenty-six primary care centers, six specialty care units, and a hospital.

In a 2009 letter to the *New England Journal of Medicine*, Dr. Eric B. Larson, executive director of the Group Health Research Institute, said that Group Health's success wasn't necessarily tied to consumer governance. It is the result of accountability built into its charter. It was designed as a prepaid group practice, and that gives its salaried doctors incentive to provide the most appropriate care to patients and keep them healthy, he wrote.

In a sense, Larson wrote, Group Health is less like a cooperative and more like "accountable care organizations" that are now being developed by insurers in response to health care reform.

New Law Sparks Growth of Accountable Care Organizations

Faced with growing pressure for better quality and less expensive medical care, the government included in the new health care law provisions for creating accountable care organizations (ACOs). Many insurers are getting involved with the formation of these new health care delivery systems.

An ACO is simply a group of health providers—such as primary care doctors, specialists, and hospitals—that is held accountable for the medical care it delivers to a group of patients. Under the new health care law, patients could end up in an ACO if most of the doctors, hospitals, and other providers they use are part of the organization. It shouldn't affect a patient's choice of doctors or other providers.

The goal of these organizations is to efficiently coordinate care. They generally operate with goals for cost containment and quality. If they meet the goals, members of the ACO often get a bonus; if they don't meet goals, they may be financially penalized.

The idea is to bridge gaps in the nation's system of fragmented health care—just another way of saying that we need to better coordinate care between independently operating hospitals, rehab facilities, nursing homes, and physicians. ACOs place critical decisions about patients in the hands of providers, who are best suited to consider the cost and quality of care.

We'll talk more about ACOs in the next chapter, which discusses the impact that health care reform is having on medicine.

Coming Next

The new health care law changes many of the old ways of practicing medicine, particularly when it comes to payment plans. Health care reform links fees to quality of care, and links quality of care to evidence-based practice. That, and more, including how the medical industry plans to deal with millions of new patients, is covered in the next chapter.

6

New Medicine

Law Attacks Errors and Inefficiencies

The American health care system struggles with serious problems.

Medical errors kill an alarming number of patients. Rising costs routinely outpace inflation. Coordination of a fragile patient's care can easily break down between a multitude of independent specialists, hospitals, nursing homes, rehabilitation centers, and home health agencies. In many areas, there are shortages of primary care doctors. And patients, along with their families, can be overwhelmed by a complicated system of care.

Now, health care reform arrives, and expects to add up to 32 million new patients to a system already trembling under its load. It's difficult to say whether the new law will solve any of the persistent problems of American medicine, or add to them. But people who made the new law knew about the problems, and they included provisions to make medicine more safe, efficient, affordable, and accessible.

For example, as mandated by the law, the US Department of Health and Human Services (HHS) in March 2011 released its National Strategy for Quality Improvement in Health Care, and it set the following priorities:

- Reduce harm to patients caused by the delivery of care.

- Ensure patients and families are engaged in care.

- Promote communication and coordination of care.

- Promote best prevention and treatment practices for leading causes of death, starting with cardiovascular disease.

- Work with communities to promote healthy living.

- Make quality care more affordable through new methods of delivering health services.

In this chapter, we'll take a look at some of these issues and more.

Attempting to Stop a Deadly Toll Taken by Medical Errors

The Patient Protection and Affordable Care Act of 2010 arrived on the tenth anniversary of the report, "To Err is Human: Building a Safer Health System." Published in 2000 by the prestigious Institute of Medicine, this hallmark study of studies sounded the alarm over medical mistakes.

The report estimated that between 44,000 and 98,000 patients die every year in US hospitals because of medical errors such as giving the wrong medicine, dosage, or treatment. Further studies have shown that over the past decade, safety conditions for patients have not improved dramatically, and some studies indicate that the problem may be worse than originally reported, especially if mistakes like preventable infections are added to the deadly mix.

Thus, medical errors remain a leading cause of death. Figure 6-1 is from the original report and essentially remains accurate in showing how the death toll from medical errors rivals other leading causes of death.

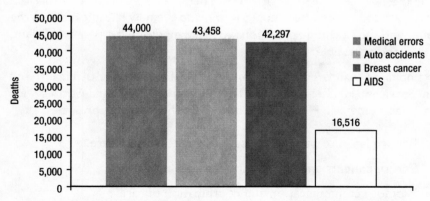

Deaths Due to Medical Errors in Hospitals Are Higher Than Certain Other Causes of Death in the U.S.

Source: The Institute of Medicine (IOM), *To Err is Human: Building a Safer Health System.* (Washington, D.C. National Academy Press, 2000.)

Note: Rates of death for cause other than medical error are from the CDC, National Center for Health Statistics, Births and Deaths: Preliminary Data for 1998, National Vital Statistics Reports. 47(25)6, 1999, as cited in *To Err is Human.*

Figure 6-1. This chart uses the low end of an estimate that indicates between 44,000 and 98,000 patients die annually from medical errors in US hospitals. Source: General Accounting Office.

In 2008, Medicare instituted a raft of safety policies in an attempt to lower the rate of medical errors, and the new health care law builds on that foundation. Officials hope private insurers follow the lead of Medicare.

The following describes some of the changes planned:

- Hospitals will get better payments for better outcomes related to the care of strokes and heart attacks, and the prevention of infections.

- Hospitals will get reduced payments for high rates of hospital-acquired conditions such as infections, bedsores, and falls.

- Medicare will track hospital error rates and in 2014 will cut payments by 1 percent to hospitals with the most problems.

- Medicare will publish each hospital's medical error track record.

- A new Patient-Centered Outcomes Research Institute will recommend the most effective treatments.

- The Center for Quality Improvement and Patient Safety will study ways to improve patient safety.

- The federal government will spend $75 million annually to improve ways to measure medical quality and safety.

TEN TIPS FOR AVOIDING DEADLY MEDICAL ERRORS

Medical errors can occur anywhere in the health care system, and there are ways to avoid them. The following tips are offered by the Agency for Healthcare Research and Quality:

- The most important thing you can do is become active in managing your health care. Get involved, ask questions, and participate in discussions. If you have a concern, speak up. Research your conditions.

- Ensure that your doctor knows what medications you are taking, and allergies and adverse reactions you have had to drugs.

- When your doctor writes a prescription, make sure you can read it.

- Ask for information about your medicines in terms that you can understand.

- If you have a choice, choose a hospital at which many patients have the procedure or surgery you need.

- While in the hospital, consider asking health care workers if they have washed their hands. Preventable infections run rampant through many hospitals, largely because of lapses in hand sanitation.

- If you are being hospitalized or undergoing an outpatient procedure, have someone accompany you as an advocate.

- If you have a test, don't assume that no news is good news. Find out results.

- If you are having surgery, make sure you, your doctor, and your surgeon agree on exactly what will be done.

- Understand that more is not always better. Find out why a treatment or test is needed. You might be better off without it.

Health Care Law Tries to Lower Hospital Readmission Rates

In a related issue, studies have shown that some hospitals have high rates of patients being readmitted shortly after being discharged, and many experts believe that is an indication of substandard care.

Figure 6-2 shows readmission rates in a recent study of Medicare fee-for-service programs.

In an attempt to shame hospitals into better performance, the Centers for Medicare & Medicaid Services in 2009 began posting 30-day readmission rates for many patients on its Hospital Compare web site at www.medicare.gov.

Health care reform takes the issue a step further by adjusting hospital payments on the basis of readmission rates in excess of what would be normally expected. In accordance with the new law, Medicare officials were preparing to begin penalizing hospitals in October 2012 with higher-than-expected readmission rates.

Despite improvements that hospitals implemented in 2011, officials reported in the summer of 2012 that very little progress was made in lowering readmission rates. However, some of the data that led to that conclusion could be a statistically misleading since federal health officials calculate

Rehospitalizations After Discharge from the Hospital Among Patients
in Medicare Fee-for-Service Programs

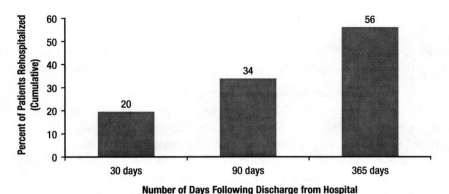

Figure 6-2. More than half of the patients in the Medicare fee-for-service program were readmitted to the hospital within a year after discharge, a trend that raises concerns about substandard care. Source: The Commonwealth Fund, adapted from "Rehospitalization Among Patients in the Medicare Fee-for Service Program," *New England Journal of Medicine*, April 2, 2009.

readmission rates over a three-year period. Thus, just one year of improvement may not accurately reflect how well hospitals are doing with this challenge. The data is published on Medicare's hospital/health care facility comparisons web site at https://data.medicare.gov.

Some medical authorities believe that penalizing hospitals for high readmission rates may be going too far. They say high readmission rates may be more the product of hospitals dealing with a high portion of impoverished patients who have poor overall health and little access to medical care needed to keep them out of hospitals. They say linking hospital readmission rates to payments may be oversimplifying a complex issue, and penalizing hospitals that are actually doing a good job of serving their communities.

In addition to readmission rate penalties, which can total 3 percent of Medicare reimbursements, other aspects of the new law, such as Medicare's Value-Based Purchasing Program, use incentives to encourage hospitals to lower readmission rates.

Fostering Better Coordination of Care, Communication

The new health care law encourages the development of better ways to coordinate care between the many types of medical providers. Studies have shown that this can save money by eliminating duplication of services and hospital readmissions. Good coordination of care also improves patient satisfaction.

Good coordination of care requires effective communications, and reimbursement systems that reward providers for working together, instead of paying them by procedure, thus encouraging medical quantity over quality.

One key to improving communications between health care providers is the electronic medical record. In 2009, Congress and the Obama Administration passed the Health Information Technology for Economic and Clinical Health Act, or HITECH. This law provides incentives through Medicare and Medicaid to clinicians and hospitals for using electronic health records. It is providing $27 billion over ten years to jumpstart the nation's electronic health records system. The law ties incentives to advances in health care processes and outcomes. These electronic systems will be used to e-prescribe drugs, measure clinical quality, gather data for studies, and share data between health professionals.

Again, the federal government is using its Medicare program to leverage electronic health records into widespread use. Hospitals and health professionals that fail to demonstrate "meaningful use" of an electronic health records system by 2015 will be penalized by Medicare. The federal government started an incentive program in May 2011 to encourage practitioners and hospitals to adopt systems. Information is available at www.cms.gov/ ehrincentiveprograms.

"Medical Home" Shifts Focus from Procedures to Patients

The new health care law includes development money for a number of payment reforms intending put more focus on providing the best patient care and less focus on multiple medical procedures. One concept that is receiving much attention is called the medical home.

The US Department of Veterans Affairs (VA) is already moving toward the medical home model for its outpatient clinics, and the American Academy of Pediatrics has been working with the concept since 1967. For example, Children's Hospital in Columbus, Ohio, has a system that cares for 285,000 children on Medicaid.

In a medical home system, treatment is coordinated by a primary care physician who maintains an ongoing relationship with patients. The doctor is supported by top information technology, a team of health professionals, and treatment guidelines based upon solid research. One key member of the team, a non-physician care manager, often guides patients to medical services such as specialists, hospitals, home health agencies, and nursing homes.

Pilot projects have shown that the medical home system can greatly reduce hospitalizations and emergency room visits while substantially cutting medical costs and improving care.

The medical home has been used to provide care to patients with chronic diseases, and payments are often made to providers on a per person, per month basis. There are incentives for meeting quality and efficiency goals.

Patients are given better access to doctors, nurses, and other providers through flexible scheduling and communications technology, such as e-mail or an interactive web site. There are systems for accepting and encouraging feedback from patients.

Creating a medical home system is expensive since it involves new technology, such as an electronic health record and a multi-disciplinary care team. Starting in 2011, the federal government began providing financial support to states that enrolled chronically ill Medicaid recipients into medical home systems.

The Affordable Care Act is helping to spread the concept. For example, in August 2012, the Community Oncology Alliance of New Mexico received a $19 million Health Care Innovation Award, a program made possible by health care reform. The money will be used to test a medical home model of care for Medicare and Medicaid beneficiaries diagnosed with breast, lung, or colorectal cancer. It is estimated that the three-year program will save $34 million in health care costs.

DIRECT PAY PRACTICES GET MEDICAL HOME STATUS

At the prodding of politicians in the state of Washington, a new trend in health care called direct pay practices was included in health care reform under the provision for medical homes.

Washington State passed legislation in 2007 that encouraged innovative pay arrangements between doctors and patients. The result was a crop of medical practices that charge each patient between $85 and $135 a month for access to primary care. Some patients have other insurance for more extensive and expensive health problems.

For instance, at Qliance Medical Management in Seattle, an older patient may pay about $80 a month for unlimited access to primary care doctors and nurse practitioners. In addition, this type of patient will likely pay another $250 or so a month for a catastrophic medical care plan with a high deductible to handle serious hospitalizations.

Qliance clinics are open weekends, and patients can contact doctors by phone or e-mail. Patients must pay for services outside the office such as lab tests, but there are usually deep discounts.

All this boils down to lower out-of-pocket costs for patients, particularly those managing a chronic illnesses like diabetes. And doctors earn more than their counterparts in standard insurance-based practices.

When state-based insurance exchanges open in 2014, they will be allowed to provide coverage through this type of plan if it meets medical home requirements.

Accountable Care Organizations Quickly Gain Ground

As I said in the previous chapter, an ACO is another type of medical organization that focuses more on patients than procedures. It is made up of a group of health providers that serves a specific group of patients. Providers often receive a single "global" payment for a patient, and then seek more efficient ways to deliver care. If successful, they are rewarded with a portion of the savings.

By July 2012, a total of 154 accountable care organizations, or ACOs, were participating in Medicare's Shared Savings Program, another provision of health care reform. These ACOs were serving about 2.4 million Medicare patients. Many of these ACOs were associated with large medical institutions and practices, but about half were physician driven and served fewer than 10,000 beneficiaries, an indication that smaller organizations are also arising out of this model for care. Thirty-two organizations were testing the Pioneer ACO Model, which was developed by the Center for Medicare and Medicaid Innovation, another product of the Affordable Care Act.

Meanwhile, a June 2012 study by Leavitt Partners, a health care consulting firm, found 221 ACOs operating, with growth concentrated in larger cities and 45 states. Many of the organizations served Medicare patients, but others were private groups, sponsored by hospitals, large physician practices, and insurance companies. Many called themselves ACOs, but some did not.

The model was also spreading to state Medicaid programs. For example, in Camden, New Jersey, one of the most impoverished and violent municipalities in the nation, the Camden Coalition of Healthcare Providers created an ACO as a Medicaid demonstration project. The coalition uses "hot spotters" to focus on patients who overutilize the medical system.

Dr. Jeffrey Brenner, a primary care physician with the coalition, cited studies that show:

- 30 percent of health care costs are run up by 1 percent of patients

- 80 percent of health care costs are run up by 13 percent of patients

- 90 percent of health care costs are run up by 20 percent of patients

The coalition found that it could generate saving in medical costs and raise the quality of care by focusing on patients who constantly go in and out of the hospital. Health coaches visit patients upon discharge, assess needs, and even accompany patients' medical appointments. They help with medications and planning appointments to ensure that patients go to the right doctors for the right treatments.

Brenner said the system works, but it must be developed from the grassroots level with providers, patients, churches, and community leaders involved. "Health care is not going to change on its own," he said. "It needs external pressure."

But there are concerns about ACOs getting too big and too powerful. The *Journal of the American Medical Association*, or *JAMA*, published a commentary on February 9, 2011, warning that hospital-centered ACOs may prove to be problematic in creating health monopolies, and a more sound approach may be to form ACOs around multi-specialty physician practices and associations. That commentary was authored by legal and medical experts from Duke University.

There are complicated issues about whether increasing cooperation between independent health care entities could foster collusion and actually increase medical costs. On November 2, 2011, the Office of the Inspector General for the Centers for Medicare & Medicaid Services issued an interim final rule that established waivers on certain federal anti-kickback laws. And about the same time, the Federal Trade Commission and Department of Justice issued a statement on ACOs and the enforcement of antitrust laws.

There is also Internal Revenue Service guidance regarding ACOs and tax-exempt organizations.

Summaries and links to all these documents and more are available at http:// oig.hhs.gov/compliance/accountable-care-organizations.

The final rule on the Medicare's Shared Savings Program for ACOs was published November 11, 2011. In 2012, the Centers for Medicare & Medicaid Services established 33 quality measures for ACOs, including care coordination and patient safety, appropriate use of preventive health services, and improved care for at-risk populations.

Doctor Shortages Predicted Along with Surge of Patients

The new health care law is expected to bring insurance coverage to millions of uninsured Americans, and that will mean a surge of new patients into the medical system at about the same time baby boomers hit the height of their needs for medical care.

Much of the pressure will fall upon primary care physicians, and already the nation doesn't have enough of them, particularly in rural and impoverished areas. The Association of American Medical Colleges estimates that with the increased surge of patients, the United States will have a shortage of about 63,000 primary care doctors by 2015, and the shortage will worsen through 2025.

To help deal with this, the new health care law attempts to shift some of the primary care load to nurse practitioners, train more physician assistants, and lure more doctors into primary care residencies with financial incentives. The law includes provisions that provide

- A 10 percent bonus by Medicare between 2011 and 2015 for primary care services furnished by doctors, nurse practitioners, clinical nurse specialists, and physician assistants. Bonuses are also included for primary care physicians and surgeons working in medically underserved areas and rural areas.

- $11 billion in federal funding for higher Medicaid payments to primary care doctors. Medicaid fees for primary care services have lagged Medicare fees by about a third, and the new law raises Medicaid's fee to Medicare's 2009 level for calendar years 2013 and 2014.

- $168 million for residency slots in medical schools to train 500 new primary care doctors by 2015.

- $1.5 billion to expand the National Health Service Corps. The corps uses financial incentives, such as helping repay education loans, to encourage primary care doctors, physician assistants, and nurse practitioners to work in areas of the country where there are shortages of health care providers.

- $32 million to train 600 new physician assistants.

- $15 million to operate ten nurse-managed clinics to help train nurse practitioners. The clinics will be situated in medically underserved areas and provide comprehensive primary care services.

- $5 million for states to expand their primary care workforce.

STATES WHERE PRIMARY CARE SHORTAGES WILL HIT HARDEST

A February 10, 2011, study published by the *New England Journal of Medicine* looked at a variety of factors to determine where shortages of primary care doctors would hit hardest in coming years.

The researchers, from the George Washington University Department of Health Policy, gauged the gap between primary care capacity and growing demand for these services. They found that residents in the following ten states would have the most difficultly getting access to primary care doctors:

1. Oklahoma
2. Georgia
3. Texas
4. Louisiana
5. Arkansas
6. Nevada
7. North Carolina
8. Kentucky
9. Alabama
10. Ohio

And the residents of these following ten states would have the least problem getting access to primary care:

1. Massachusetts
2. Vermont
3. District of Columbia

4. Maine

5. New York

6. Rhode Island

7. Connecticut

8. Washington

9. West Virginia

10. Delaware

The Evidence for Evidence-Based Practice

Part of health care reform's mandate is to encourage the use of treatments, medications, and devices that have been proven effective. It's called evidence-based practice, and while it can sort the medical wheat from the chaff, it can also stir up plenty of controversy if good research is not skillfully integrated with clinical expertise and patient values.

In other words, research can establish guidelines, but medicine is far too complicated to be put into cookbook form. There's much debate inside and outside American medicine about what constitutes the best treatment for a host of illnesses, and very few scientific studies provide absolutely conclusive guidance.

Add to that politics and money, and the result is what occurred in early 2011 in Washington State when the Health and Technology Assessment Committee began considering costs while determining which medical procedures to cover in financially strapped public insurance programs.

Some procedures were eliminated, and complaints rained down from doctors, patients, medical device makers, and opponents of health care reform who said the committee's actions were just a taste of things to come.

Critics of the committee said it was rationing care and limiting patient choice, and committee members said they were just trying to provide the safest, most reliable treatments at the best cost.

As a matter of fact, Medicare and private insurers already limit reimbursement for procedures, often because they are investigational or experimental. Breaking through that approval barrier can be a daunting task that requires much medical research and lobbying. For example, for many years Medicare refused to cover annual medical exams for beneficiaries. That has only changed recently with health care reform.

But these debates and decisions over coverage generally don't occur in open meetings amid a politically charged atmosphere with the focus on saving money.

Meanwhile, health care reform's new Patient-Centered Outcomes Research Institute organized in 2011 with the naming of board members and hiring of an executive director.

The institute will set research priorities, and its work will consist of both systematic reviews of existing evidence and new prospective research, including clinical trials and observational studies. The studies are certainly expected to have an impact on reimbursement, but officials are also supposed to take into consideration patient preferences and variations in medical practice.

The April 18, 2012, edition of the *Journal of the American Medical Association* includes two articles that outline the institute's vision for a more methodologically rigorous focus on patient needs.

New Law Creates and Renovates Community Health Centers

The new health care law builds on an existing network of community-based health centers that has operated for more than 40 years.

These centers are usually located in low-income communities and deliver comprehensive, preventive, and primary health care to patients, regardless of ability to pay.

More than 1,100 community health centers now operate at 7,900 sites. About half are located in rural areas. They provide care to nearly 19 million patients, often minorities, and economically disadvantaged people, as shown by Figure 6-3.

The Patient Protection and Affordable Care Act provides $1.5 billion for the major renovation of existing community health centers. It also provides $9.5 billion to create new community health centers in medically underserved areas, and to expand preventive and primary health care services at existing community health centers.

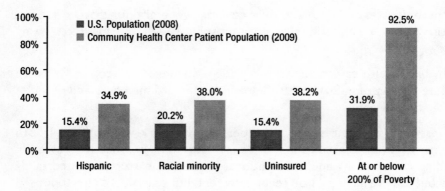

Figure 6-3. The type of patients who use community health centers. Source: US Department of Health and Human Services, Health Resources and Services Administration, 2009 Uniform Data System and US Census Bureau.

"Safety Net" Hospitals at Crossroads with Health Care Reform

Safety-net hospitals, which are often operated by local or state governments and non-profit organizations, have been relied upon by many communities for decades to provide care for low-income patients who lack insurance, but these medical institutions are kind of the odd man out with health care reform.

Many of their patients should end up being insured, either through Medicaid, which is expanding eligibility, or through new exchanges, which are offering tax credits and subsidies.

In turn, the new health care law is substantially decreasing by billions of dollars what is called "disproportionate share funding." Safety-net hospitals have been dependent upon this money, which has been provided by the government to health institutions that have cared for a "disproportionate share" of the uninsured and Medicaid beneficiaries.

However, there are now many unanswered questions about cutting off that funding, particularly if some states opt out of expanding their Medicaid coverage. The Supreme Court did not address the issue, but the ruling on Medicaid's expansion did raise concerns.

In addition, even with health care reform, government planners say that at least 23 million uninsured people will remain in America. Many of them will be undocumented immigrants so it is doubtful there will be much public support for shifting local funds to these hospitals, says Dr. Mitchell H. Katz of the San Francisco Department of Public Health.

In an article published August 11, 2010, in the *Journal of the American Medical Association,* Katz said safety net hospitals can survive if they become competitive. That means improving customer service, strengthening referral networks, and investing in technology and infrastructure.

Unfortunately, there's not going to be much money for making those improvements, Katz warns, and safety net hospitals run the risk of being left with patients excluded from health care reform, and without resources to deal with them.

Already there are concerns about the quality of care in safety-net hospitals. A study published in the July 16, 2012, issue of *Archives of Internal Medicine* found that safety-net hospitals had lower performance ratings on nearly all measures of patient satisfaction than other hospitals. The study looked at 3,096 hospitals and data from 2007 to 2010.

Coming Next

The new health care law in many way places the federal Medicare program on the cutting edge of health care reform. Medicare is growing at enormous rates, and health care reform attempts to provide better benefits while saving money. Those issues and more are examined in the next chapter.

Old Growth

Medicare at a Fiscal Crossroads

There are about 165 provisions in the Affordable Care Act that impact Medicare, the nation's insurance program for the elderly and disabled. Many of those provisions are aimed at lowering costs for the program, which in 2011 spent $549.1 billion while providing coverage for 48.7 million Americans. Even with health care reform's belt tightening, Medicare's trustees report that the program will not have enough income starting in 2024 to pay full benefits.

A good way to look at Medicare spending is as a percentage of gross domestic product, or GDP—the total value of all goods and services produced in the United States. In 2011, Medicare accounted for 3.7 percent of GDP. If something isn't done, trustees reported, it will hit 6 percent of GDP in 2040 and keep climbing. Under some scenarios, by 2080 it could exceed 10 percent of GDP. Many developed nation spend about 10 percent of GDP on their entire health care systems.

Three approaches are being advanced politically to bend the cost curve into more sustainable territory. One would turn Medicare into a program that provides subsidies to help seniors purchase private insurance—a premium-support approach. Another would maintain the existing entitlement, but trim costs and even raise the age of eligibility—a traditional fee-for-service Medicare approach. And a third would be a combination of premium support and traditional Medicare—a hybrid approach.

Medicare's growth is accelerating steadily because aging baby boomers have started hitting retirement age. Roughly 10,000 Americans a day reach age 65 and become eligible for the program. By the end of the decade, Medicare is expected to cover more than 60 million Americans, as shown in Table 7-1.

Table 7-1. A Decade of Growth: Medicare Enrollment in Millions

2009	2011	2013	2015	2017	2019
45.9	47.9	50.9	53.9	57.1	60.5

Source: Centers for Medicare & Medicaid Services.

It's important to understand that Medicare does not pay all of the medical bills for elderly and disabled Americans. The program charges monthly premiums and requires a substantial amount of cost sharing. Most beneficiaries carry supplemental insurance, or a "Medigap" policy.

Medicare has four parts:

- Part A covers hospitalization.

- Part B covers outpatient care.

- Part C consists of Medicare Advantage plans, which combine Parts A and B and are sold by private insurers.

- Part D is a drug benefit, added in 2006.

The primary source of Medicare funding is a payroll tax on covered earnings. Employers pay 1.45 percent, and their employees pay 1.45 percent. Self-employed workers pay 2.9 percent of net income.

The US Department of Health and Human Services (HHS) says the Affordable Care Act will actually lower costs for traditional Medicare beneficiaries by about $4,200 each between 2011 and 2021. The HHS says that health care reform will do that by:

- Slowing the rate of premium increases for Part B physician visits and other services

- Slowing the increase in co-payments and co-insurance required for Part A and B services

- Closing the Medicare prescription drug coverage gap, or donut hole

- Providing preventive care services to seniors at no additional cost

Medicare Attempts to Improve Quality, Control Costs

The Patient Protection and Affordable Care Act of 2010 includes a variety of measures intended to improve quality, control costs, and provide better benefits in the federal Medicare program. Overall, the new law is supposed to lower spending by $424 billion from 2010 to 2019, although it's doubtful that it will hit that mark. Medicare has a long history of planning cutbacks, and then having Congress intervene to stop the process. The provisions include:

- Payment cuts to Medicare Advantage plans. The reductions would put Medicare Advantage payments more in line, cost-wise, for the government with traditional Medicare fee-for-service plans. The cuts are being softened with a bonus program, but there have been serious questions raised about the legality of that. Details of the controversy are included later in this chapter.

- Improvements in the Medicare Part D drug benefit. As detailed in Chapter 2, the government is gradually closing the so-called "donut hole" in drug coverage, and offering discounts on brand-name drugs in the meantime. The new law also gradually lowers the spending threshold where catastrophic coverage begins, thus providing more support to beneficiaries with higher drug expenses.

- Additional preventive care services, including comprehensive annual exams, which began in 2011. There will be no out-of-pocket costs for preventive care services provided in an outpatient setting. Services include cardiovascular screenings, colorectal screenings, diabetes screenings, flu shots, mammograms, prostate screenings, and smoking cessation.

- A new Independent Payment Advisory Board to recommend ways to reduce Medicare costs if per capita spending exceeds targeted growth. The 15-member board will submit recommendations to the president and Congress, and it will be prohibited from making proposals to ration care, increase revenues, change benefits, or revamp eligibility requirements. The first recommendations are due in 2014 with implementation in 2015.

- Numerous initiatives to reduce some provider payments while increasing others, based on productivity and quality.

For example, hospitals will be penalized for high rates of infections, but rewarded for good care. This is an attempt to start basing payments on quality instead of quantity.

- New payment systems. Medicare is conducting pilot studies that combine payments for certain types of care. It is also establishing accountable care organizations (ACOs). The pilot studies are being conducted through the Center for Medicare and Medicaid Innovation, which was created by health care reform.

- Reductions in Medical Disproportionate Share Hospital payments by 25 percent. These payments are made primarily to "safety net" hospitals, and they will be reduced as more people are insured, thus lowering costs for uncompensated care. Reductions are expected to total $14 billion, but questions are being raised about that move since some states are balking at expanding their Medicaid programs, thus putting more pressure on their safety net hospitals.

- The Independence at Home demonstration program for Medicare beneficiaries with exceptional health care needs. A team of health care professionals will provide primary care services in the home, and share savings to Medicare if quality and satisfaction measures are met. The initial program is limited to 10,000 beneficiaries, and a list of 16 participating medical practices was published April 26, 2012, by the Centers for Medicare & Medicaid Services.

- A new Federal Coordinated Health Care Office to more effectively provide services to so-called "dual eligibles," people who qualify for both Medicare and Medicaid. Studies have shown that dual eligibles often run up high medical costs, which can be contained if services are better coordinated. In July 2012, officials were planning a high-profile demonstration project involving up to 2 million dual eligibles in 26 states.

- Increased surveillance and prevention of waste, fraud, and abuse. Medicare will provide more oversight and screening of providers. It is creating a database to share information with law enforcement, and it is requiring more documentation for services performed. Penalties are being enhanced for marketing and claims violations involving Medicare Advantage plans and the Part D prescription benefit. However, there are growing concerns about overlapping audits and cost-to-benefit ratios for some fraud-fighting efforts. We will discuss some of those issues later in this chapter.

- New rules requiring doctors to meet patients face-to-face before certifying them for home health services and medical equipment. These rules, which started in April 2011, were implemented to reduce fraud. They have been the subject of continuous changes. For example, the proposed 2013 Fee-for-Service Payment Schedule expands the list of medical equipment requiring a face-to-face meeting.

- New or additional monthly premiums for some enrollees. Health care reform freezes the income threshold for Part B premiums at 2010 levels, which means the number of enrollees subject to this income-related premium will rise from 2.4 million in 2011 to 7.8 million in 2019. The Affordable Care Act also established a new income-based Part D premium beginning in 2011 for individuals earning more than $85,000 and couples earning more than $170,000 a year. About 1.2 million beneficiaries were subject to the premium in 2011, and that will rise to 4.2 million beneficiaries in 2019.

- Payroll tax increase to 2.35 percent from 1.45 percent for individuals earning $200,000 or more and for couples earning $250,000 or more. This tax would also apply to some investment income for people with high incomes. More details are available in Chapter 10.

- Expansion of a controversial Competitive Bidding Program for durable medical equipment used in the home. Many authorities believe that Medicare could apply principles of this program to other sectors of health spending. Details are included later in this chapter.

Planned Cuts to Medicare Advantage Create Concern

Under health care reform, Medicare Advantage plans are scheduled for $136 billion in cuts between 2012 and 2019. Approved by Medicare, but run by private insurance companies, Medicare Advantage plans have become extremely popular in recent years; they have 11 million members. Cutting the plans' funding raises real concerns from beneficiaries and insurers.

The plans often offer lower out-of-pocket costs and better services than traditional Medicare plans. Most provide coverage under health maintenance organizations (HMOs). Unfortunately, Medicare Advantage plans cost the government more than traditional Medicare, and they often make payments to providers that are less than those made by traditional Medicare.

Figure 7-1 shows how beneficiaries are distributed in Medicare Advantage plans.

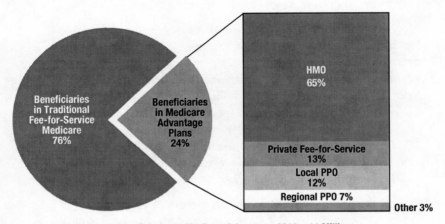

Distribution of Medicare Advantage Enrollment, by Plan Type, 2010

Total Medicare Beneficiaries in Medicare Advantage, 2010 = 11 Million

Source: Kaiser Slides, The Henry J. Kaiser Family Foundation, November 2010

Figure 7-1. The distribution of beneficiaries in different types of Medicare Advantage plans. Source: Graph by Kaiser Family Foundation with data from Mathematica Policy Research and Medicare Advantage enrollment files. This information was reprinted with permission from the Henry J. Kaiser Family Foundation.

Six Types of Medicare Advantage Plans Defined

There are six different types of Medicare Advantage plans; each is described in the following list. Most plans offer prescription drug coverage.

1. *Health Maintenance Organization (HMO):* Provides access to a network of doctors and hospitals that coordinates care, with emphasis on prevention. HMOs allow enrollees more benefits than the standard Medicare plan and many supplement plans. But they offer the most restrictive network, and prior approval is usually required for coverage of out-of-network care.

2. *Health Maintenance Organization with Point-of-Service Option (HMO-POS):* An HMO with a more flexible network that allows members to seek care outside network under some circumstances, often with higher co-pays.

3. *Medicare Medical Savings Account (MSA):* A combination of a high-deductible health plan and a bank account for the member. The plan deposits a set amount in the account annually, and the money is used to pay Medicare Part A and Part B bills. After a deductible is met, the plan pays for more Medicare-covered services. These plans lack Medicare Part D prescription coverage.

4. *Medicare Special Needs Plans (SNPs):* Offers coverage for Medicare beneficiaries with special needs and chronic conditions such as diabetes. SNPs are often restricted to people with certain medical conditions.

5. *Preferred Provider Organization (PPO):* Provides a network of doctors and hospitals to coordinate care. PPOs often provide more benefits than traditional Medicare and many supplement plans. They usually allow members to go outside network, but with higher co-pays.

6. *Private Fee-for-Service (PFFS):* Allows members to go to any doctor or hospital that accepts Medicare, along with the plan's payment schedule. The private insurer, rather than Medicare, decides fees and co-pays. These plans offer minimal savings for members, but often include benefits not offered by traditional Medicare.

New Law Attempts to Bring Medicare Advantage Costs in Line

Medicare Advantage plans provide benefits to members. The companies operating the plans receive a set amount each month from Medicare for each person, based upon a complicated bidding process. The bids have come in between 9 and 13 percent higher than the cost of Medicare's traditional fee-for-service plan.

Under health care reform, in 2012 Medicare started reducing fees paid to Medicare Advantage plans to bring costs more in line with traditional Medicare plans. Payments to Medicare Advantage will be further reduced beginning in 2014 as Medicare adjusts the method it uses to provide extra compensation for members with high-cost health care needs.

Amid rising concern about these cuts, the government in late 2010 rolled out a bonus program for Medicare Advantage plans to mitigate losses. It is based upon an existing rating system—administered by the Centers for Medicare & Medicaid Services—that rates the quality of Medicare Advantage plans. Ratings are based upon things like quality of care, responsiveness to problems, and customer satisfaction.

A five-star rating is best, but those with four stars get a bonus, too, at the following increasing levels:

- 1.5 percent increase in 2012

- 3 percent increase in 2013

- 5 percent increase in 2014

The bonus is doubled for Medicare Advantage plans operating in counties that meet certain qualifications, such as having at least 25 percent of Medicare recipients signed up in Medicare Advantage plans. In addition, Medicare has adjusted the bonus program to allow three-star programs to get bonuses on a sliding scale for three years.

In July 2012, the Government Accountability Office's General Counsel raised serious questions about the legality of the bonus program. In ten-page letter to the HHS, General Counsel Lynn Gibson said his agency was concerned about Medicare's legal authority to institute the $8.5 billion bonus program. Although the program was included in the Affordable Care Act as a quality incentive, Medicare officials may have improperly expanded the bonuses under political pressure to offset cuts to a popular service.

In addition, health care reform extends several consumer protections to people enrolled in Medicare Advantage plans. They include

- Prohibitions against Medicare Advantage plans having higher cost-sharing charges than traditional fee-for-service plans.

- Requirements that Medicare Advantage plans spend at least 85 percent of money collected from premiums on medical benefits, or else refund the difference to the government. Beginning in 2014, this is an attempt to limit administrative costs, profits, and overhead.

- Providing people enrolled in Medicare Advantage drug plans with the same improvement in coverage as that offered by closure of the so-called "donut hole."

MEDICARE ADVANTAGE ENROLLMENT PERIODS CHANGE

Medicare has changed its sign-up period for Medicare Advantage plans.

Previously, enrollments were accepted between November 15 and December 31 each year. Now, the sign-up time runs from October 15 until December 7; this began in 2011 for plan year 2012.

Beneficiaries already enrolled in Medicare Advantage plans as of January 1 of each year, beginning in 2011, will be allowed 46 days from the beginning of the calendar year to switch back to a tradition Medicare fee-for-service plan. Enrollees will not be allowed to switch from one Medicare Advantage plan to another during that time.

Affordable Care Act Attempts to Better Control Medicare Fraud

For many years, Medicare was a classic example of a giant government program highly vulnerable to fraud. The reason was pretty simple. In the past, Medicare paid health providers and suppliers before actually checking whether the bills they submitted were valid. Only after payments were made did auditors check for fraud. This "pay-and-chase" system had obvious weaknesses.

For example, for many years, a bogus supplier could simply fill out paperwork and get a Medicare billing number from the National Supplier Clearinghouse. All that was required were Medicare beneficiary numbers, so a "shell" company could bill and be paid for services and medical equipment that were never delivered. By the time auditors figured out what happened, the scam artist could be long gone with millions of dollars in Medicare payments.

Now, the government is trying to switch to a fraud-prevention system that checks the credentials of providers and suppliers more closely and uses technology developed by credit card companies to quickly identify patterns of fraud and then cut off payments. The Affordable Care Act includes numerous provisions contributing to this Medicare initiative to combat fraud. They include:

- Tools that increase the oversight of health providers and suppliers. This includes mandatory licensing checks prior to billing Medicare, and the withholding of payments when a fraud investigation starts.

- An additional $350 million (this decade) to fund the Health Care Fraud and Abuse Account.

- A provision allowing the Centers for Medicare & Medicaid Services to share data with other federal agencies.

- A requirement that providers and suppliers establish their own compliance programs for preventing, identifying, and correcting fraudulent business practices.

- Expanding authority to recover overpayments.

- Tougher penalties to deter fraud and abuse.

This is much more complicated than it seems. Because of highly publicized cases of Medicare fraud, the government has already instituted multiple layers of audits on providers and suppliers. Some providers and suppliers say that these audits, which are carried out by government contractors, can be arbitrary, overlapping, and burdensome.

In 2012, the Senate Finance Committee began investigating these complaints, along with troubling reports from the General Accountability Office and Office of the Inspector General about Medicare's attempts to improve its fraud-fighting capabilities. In a July 31, 2012, letter to the Centers for Medicare & Medicaid Services, Senator Orrin Hatch (R-UT) and Senator Tom Coburn (R-OK) raised questions about the agency spending $77 million on a computer system to predict fraudulent billing patterns. The senators expressed concern about the system's limited capabilities and reluctance by Medicare officials to discuss its problems and limitations.

Nonetheless, Medicare unveiled a new $3.6 million fraud command center on August 1, 2012, featuring the new technology developed largely through provisions in the Affordable Care Act.

The issue becomes even more complex when fraud, abuse, and waste are all mixed together by Medicare's extremely complicated coding system for billing providers and suppliers. For example, government auditors routinely find coding error rates of 90 percent or greater when closely examining documentation for purchases billed to Medicare. That error rate can be easily confused with rates of fraud, abuse, and waste, but these errors are often clerical. In addition, many of Medicare's complicated documentation requirements are subject to wide interpretation, creating even more confusion about what exactly constitutes fraud, waste, and abuse.

Affordable Care Act Expands Competitive Bidding Program

In an effort to lower costs, Congress in 2003 created a Competitive Bidding Program to be used by Medicare to purchase home care items like wheelchairs, beds, and diabetic testing supplies. Phase I of the Competitive Bidding Program targeted nine metropolitan areas thought to be hotspots for fraud by suppliers of durable medical equipment. Prices and contracts went into effect in 2010, and the Affordable Care Act helped expand the program into 91 additional metropolitan areas, with contracts and prices scheduled to start in July 2013.

Depending on how it is viewed, Medicare's Competitive Bidding Program was either a huge success or a huge failure in the nine areas where it has been in effect long enough to measure outcomes. Medicare claims the program saved the agency $202 million its first year, and eliminated fraud, waste, and abuse. It did that by forcing a consolidation of the home medical equipment industry. Hundreds of mom-and-pop operations were forced out of business because they couldn't handle high volumes of products and low margins. That left a few large providers widely spread over large metropolitan areas.

Of greater concern was a sharp decline in claims for home medical equipment used by Medicare beneficiaries. For example, sales of standard power wheelchairs declined by 81.5 percent in the affected areas, according to an analysis by Peter Crampton, a University of Maryland economist. Crampton said that by disrupting referral networks and creating geographical obstacles, the competitive bidding process made home medical equipment more difficult for beneficiaries to obtain. Therefore, claims plummeted.

Crampton and other auction experts also sharply criticized Medicare for design flaws in its Competitive Bidding Program. Normally, competitive bidding requires suppliers to submit binding bids, but Medicare allowed providers to submit non-binding, low-ball bids. Essentially, auction experts said, Medicare inadvertently created an unsustainable bidding system that will lead to industry collapse and monopolies.

Medicare spending for durable medical equipment only accounts for about 1.5 percent of its budget, but the Competitive Bidding Program demonstrates what the government can do when it exercises its muscle in the market. Also, Medicare officials have said they eventually hope to apply competitive bidding principles to other types of goods and services.

Coming Next

The US Supreme Court's ruling on health care reform created much confusion and controversy over plans to expand Medicaid, the nation's program for insuring low-income people. In the next chapter, we'll look at what the Affordable Care Act had planned for Medicaid, and how the ruling changed that.

Backlash

Ruling Slows Medicaid Expansion

On June 28, 2012, the US Supreme Court released a mixed ruling on the Patient Protection and Affordable Care Act of 2010. The court upheld the law's individual mandate. But it placed limits on another key provision of the law—the expansion of Medicaid, a program that provides states with funding to pay medical bills for pregnant women, children, needy families, and the disabled.

The court ruled that the federal government could not force states to expand Medicaid by threatening to cut off existing funding for the program. Medicaid and its associated Children's Health Insurance Program (CHIP) provided health insurance coverage in 2012 to about 63 million Americans.

For many years, states have managed Medicaid programs and have been allowed to set their own eligibility standards as long as programs covered pregnant women and young children living below 133 percent of the poverty level. Thus, income standards for parents varied widely among states, and ranged from 11 to 400 percent of the poverty level. Forty-two states excluded all adults without children or a disability, despite low income levels.

The Affordable Care Act attempted to expand Medicaid by setting a national eligibility standard at 133 percent of the poverty level for all individuals and families, starting in 2014. Eligibility would be based on modified adjusted gross income, which includes total income plus tax-exempt interest and foreign earned income. A special 5 percent adjustment to the formula essentially would put the eligibility level at 138 percent of the poverty level.

If applied to all states, that change would add more than 16 million Americans to Medicaid, mostly low-income, childless adults without disability. The Affordable Care Act had been using a carrot-or-stick approach to encourage the expansion.

First, there was the stick. If states refused to expand the program, the federal government would cut off all existing funding for Medicaid. It was an all-or-nothing deal, and no state appeared willing to sacrifice their existing Medicaid program to avoid the expansion.

Then, there was the carrot. Normally, states are required to pay matching funds to the federal government for Medicaid money. On average, states pay 43 percent of costs, although the match varies widely among states and depends largely upon poverty levels. To encourage expansion, the federal government planned to cover all the costs for new beneficiaries from 2014 through 2016. After that, states would be required to provide a match that would rise to 10 percent of funding by 2020 and subsequent years.

In siding with states that sued over the issue, the court appeared to have no problem with the carrot, but ruled that the stick was unconstitutional. The court noted that a spending clause in the Constitution allows Congress to pay debts and establish "cooperative" programs with states. The threat to cut off existing Medicaid funding amounted to "economic dragooning," and therefore, was considered unconstitutional, the court ruled. This opened the door for states to opt out of the expansion.

Court Ruling Creates New Choices for States

Giving states the option whether or not to participate in the Medicaid expansion may seem simple, but it's pretty complicated because of other provisions of health care reform.

Immediately after the ruling, governors of six states threatened to opt out of the Medicaid expansion. Even if state contributions would be minimal, governors say they were balking at the expansion of Medicaid because they were concerned about the rising costs of all government programs. They noted that the federal government is already grappling with budget deficits, and there's a good possibility that the financial burden for the expansion eventually would be transferred to states, which also are wrestling with budget problems.

States opting out of the Medicaid expansion would leave large numbers of low-income Americans out of health care reform's stronger and tighter health insurance safety net. Those excluded would be people with incomes between 0 and 138 percent of the poverty level. Some people could go to insurance exchanges for help since exchanges offer premium support to individuals and families with incomes between 100 and 400 percent of the poverty level; but that's only a small portion—those with incomes between 100 and 138 percent of the poverty level.

People with lower incomes—between 0 and 100 percent of the poverty level—would be left without any assistance. So in the summer of 2012, some policymakers were exploring the possibility of states setting Medicaid eligibility for individuals and families with income levels at or below 100 percent of the poverty rate. That would fill the gap.

If allowed by the federal government, however, that approach would produce still another consequence. It would push more people into exchanges to purchase insurance that is more expensive than Medicaid, and it requires some cost sharing. A report from the Congressional Budget Office in July 2012 estimated that it would cost the federal government about $6,000 a year for every new Medicaid enrollee. The cost for a low-income enrollee in exchanges would be about $9,000 a year.

Medicaid and its associated CHIP program are already planning to coordinate services with the health insurance exchanges that will be operating in each state. Among other things, people will be able to sign up for Medicaid at those exchanges through a streamlined and upgraded system that determines eligibility.

In its July 2012 report, the Congressional Budget Office also projected that some states would completely opt out of the Medicaid expansion, some would expand in 2014, and some would enact partial expansions. However, much would depend upon how flexible federal officials are in allowing variations from the original language in the Affordable Care Act.

According to the report, the key questions remaining to be answered by the federal government include:

- Will states be allowed to expand their Medicaid programs after 2014?

- Will states be allowed to set eligibility thresholds below 138 percent of the poverty level?

- Will states be allowed to fill gaps in coverage by extending Medicaid eligibility to "reasonable categories" of individuals, as allowed by existing provisions in Medicaid rules?

On August 6, 2012, an official with the Centers for Medicare & Medicaid Services indicated that the federal government was leaning toward more flexibility in implementing the Medicaid expansion. Speaking at a Chicago conference of state legislatures, the spokesperson said states could opt into the expansion, but then opt out later.

Overall, the Congressional Budget Office report calculated that the Supreme Court ruling will result in 6 million fewer children and adults being covered by Medicaid in 2022. That will add up to an $84 billion savings for the federal government between 2012 and 2022, the Congressional Budget Office estimated.

TEXAS: A STATE OF CONTRADICTIONS

Texas Governor Rick Perry quickly responded to the June 28, 2012, Supreme Court ruling. He announced on July 9 that his state would opt out of the Affordable Care Act's expansion of Medicaid.

That raised some eyebrows and plenty of skepticism about Perry's ability to follow through on his decision. There are several reasons why.

Texas has one of the nation's highest rates of uninsured residents. About 26 percent of Texans have no health insurance. That's about 6.3 million people. There are already 1.8 million Texans enrolled in Medicaid, and the expansion would add another 1.4 million residents to the program, substantially lowering its rate of uninsured residents.

Expanding Medicaid would bring a huge amount of money into the Texas health care system. The Kaiser Family Foundation estimated that it would amount to $55.1 billion in federal spending and $2.6 billion in state spending between 2014 and 2019.

Texas is home to some very well-known medical centers, and turning down the Medicaid expansion would be taking money out of their pockets. The Texas Hospital Association has already expressed support for the Medicaid expansion.

Texas is also home to some very powerful managed care companies that would profit from a Medicaid expansion. Texas has already received a waiver that allows it to expand its Medicaid managed care system early, in anticipation of the expansion.

And the same day that Perry announced that Texas would opt out of the expansion, WellPoint, Inc. disclosed an agreement to purchase Amerigroup Corp., the largest Medicaid managed care provider in Texas. Combined, those companies will manage Medicaid plans that serve 4.5 million beneficiaries in 19 states.

Nobody expects anything to change politically until after the November election, but after that, many think the big talk of politicians will shrink.

Other New Standards Apply to State Medicaid Programs

Setting a national standard for eligibility, however, does not mean that all Medicaid programs will be identical. There will remain wide variation, beyond eligibility, in how states administer programs. But there are other new standards for Medicaid included in health care reform.

Newly eligible adults must receive coverage that equals the minimum essential health benefits package offered in the new insurance exchanges. That includes prescription drug and mental health coverage. However, states are not required to offer Medicaid recipients the long list of preventive care services that is being mandated for all other new insurance policies. But if states do offer that coverage, they will receive a 1 percent funding increase from the federal government.

In addition, states are required to maintain eligibility levels for Medicaid and the CHIP through September 30, 2019. This prevents financially troubled states from limiting or cutting access to the program. Essentially, it is causing a further increase in enrollees.

MANY STATES RECEIVE MEDICAID WAIVERS

For years, federal officials have issued Section 115 Medicaid demonstration waivers that provide states with flexibility in operating programs. There have been several of these waivers issued to states since the Affordable Care Act was enacted.

As of May 2012, Medicaid waivers have been granted to:

- Seven states so that they can expand Medicaid early to adults.

- Two states so that they can streamline enrollment processes for adults.

- Four states so that they can temporarily restrict enrollment because of financial constraints.

- Four states so that they can require high-need beneficiaries to enroll in a managed care plan. Two states have received waivers so they can expand managed care systems.

- Four states so that they can receive federal matching funds to cover uncompensated care and improve medical care delivery systems. In addition, five states have received waivers so that they can implement improvements in medical care delivery systems, such as medical or health homes.

Meanwhile, Vermont is embarking on an ambitious plan to create a unified health care system to achieve the benefits of a single-payer system, and it needs numerous waivers from provisions of the Affordable Care Act, including those affecting its Medicaid program.

Massachusetts, another state enacting its own health care reform, is also operating under large-scale waivers of Medicaid rules.

In 2011, President Obama opened the door for more states to enact their own types of health care reform. He offered to grant states waivers from the Affordable Care Act's provisions in 2014. However, states must demonstrate that their plans are budget neutral and they must provide the same level of coverage as the Affordable Care Act.

A policy brief from the Kaiser Commission on Medicaid and the Uninsured noted that at least 34 states were operating with some form of a Medicaid waiver in May 2012.

New Support Encouraging Baby Boomers to "Age in Place"

Medicaid pays more than 40 percent of the bill for all long-term care in the United States, with more than a million nursing home residents relying upon the program. But institutional care is expensive, and in recent years, Medicaid has been creating services that allow older people to live at home longer and stay out of institutional care, as shown in Figure 8-1.

Over the past decade, government funding for institutionally based long-term care has grown at an average annual rate of 6.3 percent, compared with 11.8 percent for community-based long-term care and services.

Health care reform builds on this trend by offering more support for people to "age in place" as baby boomers move into their final, fragile years and threaten to swamp social services. Provisions include:

- Options that allow states to offer home and community-based services through a Medicaid State Plan Amendment rather than through individual waivers. Began October 1, 2010.

- The Community First Choice Option, which allows states to provide community-based support and services to people with incomes up to 150 percent of the federal poverty level, and who have disabilities normally requiring institutional care.

Growth in Medicaid Long-Term Care Expenditures, 1990-2008

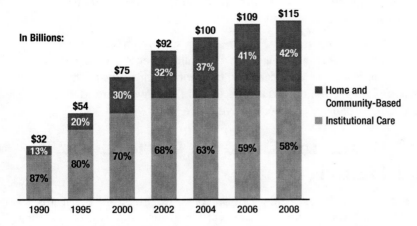

Note: Home and community-based care includes home health, personal care services and home and community-based service waivers.
Source: Kaiser Slides, The Henry J. Kaiser Family Foundation, July 2010

Figure 8-1. Nursing home costs have peaked in the United States, while home and community-based care costs have grown. Medicaid has encouraged this trend because it saves money, and people usually prefer their homes to institutional care—if they can manage. Source: This information was reprinted with permission from the Henry J. Kaiser Family Foundation.

States are providing an additional 6 percentage points of matching funds for the program. The overall cost is expected to hit $6 billion over a decade.

- The State Balancing Incentive Program, which provides $3 billion to eligible states for increasing long-term care services that are not based in institutions. Began October 1, 2010.

- Funds to continue initiatives by the Aging and Disability Resource Centers program ($10 million per year from 2010 through 2014). This collaborative effort between the Administration on Aging and the Centers for Medicare & Medicaid Services is designed to streamline access to long-term care services and supports. In August 2012, a federal official testified to a US Senate Committee that Aging and Disability Resource Centers were operating in 200 sites in all 50 states.

- Protections against spousal impoverishment for people receiving Medicaid home and community-based services. Begins in 2014, and runs for five years.

- The Money Follows the Person program, which provides long-term services and supports that allow beneficiaries to move out of institutional care and back into their homes. The program was scheduled to expire in 2011, but was extended by the Affordable Care Act for five more years.

New Options for Chronic Conditions, Mental Health

Health care reform includes a new option for state Medicaid programs to implement "health homes" for patients with chronic conditions, including mental illnesses. It is also funding a demonstration project to improve emergency care for psychiatric patients.

Under health care reform, the federal government provides states with 90 percent of funding for a health home program during the first two years that the State Plan Amendment is in place.

Under health care reform, the federal government provides states with 90 percent of funding for a health home program during the first two years that a health home State Plan Amendment is in place. As of August 2012, 20 states had expressed an interest in the program, and six states had received federal approval for their plans.

The health home concept seeks to better integrate primary, acute, and mental health care, along with long-term care services and support.

To be eligible for the program, patients must have two chronic conditions, have one chronic condition and be at risk for another, or have one serious and persistent mental health condition.

Chronic conditions listed in the new law include mental health problems, substance abuse, asthma, diabetes, heart disease, and obesity. Other chronic conditions, such as HIV/AIDS, may be added to the list, federal officials reported.

Health home services include comprehensive care management, care coordination, comprehensive transitional care, patient and family support, and use of health technology to link services.

The Affordable Care Act also includes up to $75 million in funding over three years for a Medicaid Emergency Demonstration Project in the District of

Columbia and 11 states—Alabama, California, Connecticut, Illinois, Maine, Maryland, Missouri, North Carolina, Rhode Island, Washington, and West Virginia.

The project is focusing on the problem of psychiatric patients ending up in general hospital emergency departments, where they often have difficulty getting appropriate care and create delays for other patients.

Medicaid is paying fees for treating psychiatric emergencies in psychiatric hospital settings. Normally, Medicaid does not reimburse psychiatric institutions for this care, a restriction known as Medicaid's IMD exclusion.

Medicaid Fee Increases for Primary Care Doctors Set for 2013, 2014

For many years, medical fees paid to primary care doctors to care for Medicaid patients have lagged behind those paid for Medicare patients. This has led to reluctance by some doctors to accept Medicaid patients. In fact, an August 2012 study published in the journal *Health Affairs* found that nearly one-third of US physicians said they would not accept new Medicaid patients because of the low fees.

The Affordable Care Act contains a provision to raise Medicaid payments to primary care doctors to Medicare levels for calendar years 2013 and 2014. A proposed rule on the increase was published in May 2012.

The higher fees will go to doctors in family medicine, general internal medicine, pediatric medicine, and related subspecialties. The fee increase is expected to cost $11 billion, and will be paid for by the federal government.

Some doctors remain reluctant to accept Medicaid patients even if fees are raised. They point out that the increase has been funded for only two years, and they don't want to accept patients and then later have Medicaid lower fees back to previous levels.

Coming Next

The new health care law is packed with promises that consumers will get more information about medicine—much more information. That could prove to be challenging since most Americans are already easily confounded by too much medical minutiae. The law even gives us more information about our food—with a provision requiring restaurants and vending machines to provide nutritional labels. We'll look those communication issues and more in the next chapter.

Info Overload

Law Brings Communication Challenges

The new health care law promises to bestow upon us much more information about the American medical system, or as government planners say, make it more transparent.

There will be details about a host of new insurance options, all with their own deductibles and vast array of new benefits. We'll have new data about medical errors, hospital infection rates, and quality measures for hospitals and other health providers. Of course, all this will be available at our fingertips, on the Internet.

Add that to the existing complexities of medical care, including all the specialists, therapeutic guidance, technology, and prescription drugs, each with a brand and a generic name.

It really will be way too much for many to comprehend. People already struggle with health literacy, and adding more information could make it worse.

In this short chapter, we'll look at the problem of health literacy, and some of the ways health care reform approaches it. We'll also look at new sources of health information, a new requirement that drug companies disclose financial ties to doctors, and new nutritional labeling standards for restaurants and vending machines.

Only 1 in 8 Americans Proficient in Health Literacy

A November 2010 study commissioned by the Institute of Medicine, "Health Literacy Implications of the Affordable Care Act," notes that 36 percent of American adults are functionally illiterate. They may have some education, but for all practical purposes, they are unable to write a sentence or read a book. Only 12 percent of Americans adults have proficient health literacy, meaning they can readily understand health information and use it to follow a doctor's orders, grasp a diagnosis, or adhere to dosing directions for a prescription.

Many provisions of health care reform are aimed specifically at helping low-income people, including up to 16 million new enrollees for Medicaid. That group includes a significant portion of Americans who lack education, and certainly, like many people who are very well educated, they are easily baffled by medical concepts and terminology. To really complicate things, consider the challenges of communicating new, detailed information about health care reform to people who are elderly and lack computer skills.

Research shows that health literacy does matter. A study released March 28, 2011, by the Agency for Healthcare Research and Quality found that low health literacy in older Americans was linked to poorer health and a higher risk of death. The study noted that more than 75 million English-speaking adults in the United States have extremely limited health literacy. The study also found a link between low health literacy and more frequent use of hospital emergency rooms and inpatient care.

Health literacy varies widely in America. It is influenced by culture or race, as shown by Figure 9-1 from a 2003 study.

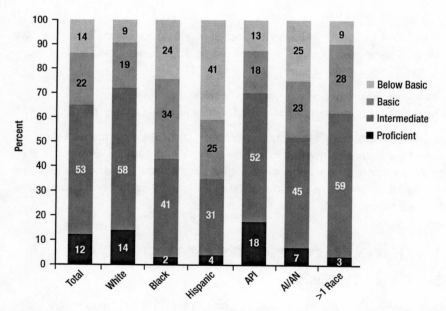

Figure 9-1. The distribution of adult health literacy levels by race and ethnicity, 2003. API=Asian or Pacific Islander; AI/AN=American Indian or Alaska Native. Source: National Assessment of Adult Literacy, Health Literacy Component, 2003.

Figure 9-1's legend items are described as follows:

- *Below Basic*: No more than the most simple and concrete skills, such as circling the date of a medical appointment.

- *Basic*: Skills necessary for simple and everyday activities, such as understanding a clearly written pamphlet.

- *Intermediate*: Skills necessary for moderately challenging activities, such using the information on a label to identify three substances that may interact with an over-the-counter drug and cause side effects.

- *Proficient*: Skills necessary for more complex and challenging activities, such as finding the meaning of a medical term to help manage health and prevent disease.

Law Attempts to Bridge Communication Chasm

Health care reform addresses the importance of health literacy, particularly in providing consumers with information about insurance policies that will be offered through the new insurance exchanges. It requires that descriptions for these policies be written in plain language so more people can easily understand them and compare them.

The new health care law also includes the following required provisions.

- The Agency for Healthcare Research and Policy must publicize research results in ways that reach consumers with diverse levels of health literacy.

- Federal grants will be awarded to develop and update aids (information in various forms) on the safety, effectiveness, and cost of medical treatments. These aids will be designed to help health care providers educate patients and caregivers through diverse health literature.

- Consultation with experts on health literacy is required to evaluate standardized information on prescription drug labels and print advertising.

- Federal grants will be awarded to train health care providers to communicate with patients from diverse cultures and with varying degrees of health literacy.

Simplified Summary of Benefits and Coverage Required

Beginning September 23, 2012, insurance companies must provide a summary of benefits, or SBC, to participants in group health plans.

This four-page document comes in a uniform format described in final regulations issued February 14, 2012, by the US Departments of Labor, Treasury, and Health and Human Services.

The regulations include specific guidance for creating a template and for the type of language to use in the document. Information in the SBC must include:

- Description of coverage
- Exceptions and limitations on coverage
- Co-pays
- Conditions for renewing policy
- Examples of coverage
- Contact information, including an Internet address
- A glossary of health insurance terms and words

Health Care Reform Brings New Sources of Information

The new health care law includes a multitude of new sources for information. Many are Internet-based, but information also will be available through telephone, print, television, and radio.

The following are some of the main sources of new information being provided through the Patient Protection and Affordable Care Act of 2010:

- HealthCare.gov (www.healthcare.gov): The US government's primary web site for health care reform. It links to other web sites and guides people and businesses to and through the new insurance exchanges. This site also provides eligibility guidelines for all government insurance programs and subsidized private insurance. Although most state-based exchanges won't open until 2014, the site already provides links to the temporary exchanges established to help cover people with pre-existing conditions. Those sites also may be accessed through www.pcip.gov.

- Medicare.gov (www.medicare.gov): The US government web site providing information about Medicare health and drug plans, and health providers. This site has been up and running for years, but the amount of data available on it has been growing exponentially. It's not just for Medicare beneficiaries, although it may appear so. Among many features, the site has tools allowing users to compare hospital safety and performance records, and to gauge the quality of nursing homes and dialysis facilities. Users can also see how much hospitals are paid by Medicare for certain procedures. Starting in 2014, the US Department of Health and Human Services (HHS) will start publicly reporting rates of medical errors and infections for all hospitals admitting Medicare beneficiaries. That data should also be available at www.hhs.gov, another government web site packed with consumer health information. A related HHS web site at http://cciio.cms.gov contains major regulations and guidance for health care reform.

- The Health Resources and Services Administration (www.hrsa.gov). This US government web site contains information about health care reform, but its content is tailored for providers. For instance, it leads users through the application process for the National Health Service Corps, which is recruiting primary care, dental, and mental health providers to work in medically underserved communities.

- The Patient Protection and Affordable Care Act web page (www.dol.gov/ebsa/healthreform): Operated by the US Department of Labor. The site includes regulations and guidance about health care reform.

- The National Association of Insurance Commissioners (www.naic.org): This web site has some consumer resources, but it's really geared to state regulators who are deeply involved with health care reform.

In addition, there are web sites that provide up-to-date, in-depth, factual, and relatively objective information about health care reform. They include sites operated by the following nonprofit foundations:

- The Henry J. Kaiser Family Foundation (http://healthreform.kff.org)

- The Commonwealth Fund (www.commonwealthfund.org).

- The Robert Wood Johnson Foundation (www.rwjf.org).

Law Requires Disclosure of Financial Ties with Doctors

The Physician Payment Sunshine Act was included as Section 6002 of the Health Care Reform Act. It requires drug and medical device manufacturers to disclose the gifts or amount of money they give to doctors and academic medical centers.

The information must be reported to the HHS, which will publish it on a web site. The Centers for Medicare & Medicaid Services published proposed rules on December 19, 2011, and in the following 60 days received more than 300 comments from interested parties.

A final rule is expected in late 2012. However, applicable manufacturers and group purchasing organizations will not be required to collect data before January 1, 2013. Eventually, annual reports will be required.

The provisions were passed because of concern that these payments and gifts, often given for lectures, could improperly influence the types and amounts of drugs or treatments dispensed by doctors. The law just requires disclosure; there is no limit on these financial relationships.

The law requires disclosure of all payments and gifts to doctors, including food, entertainment, or gifts; travel; consulting fees; honoraria; research funding or grants; education or conference funding; stocks or stock options; ownership or investment interest; royalties or licenses; and charitable contributions.

The law exempts educational material for patients, rebates and discounts, loans of devices, items provided under warranty, dividend, or investment interests in a publicly traded security or mutual fund, and payments made to a physician who is a patient, or an employee of the reporting company. The law also exempts payments less than $10, until combined they total $100, and then they must be reported.

Also exempt are prescription drug and device samples, but another section of the new health care law requires that samples be reported to the HHS.

Health Care Law Requires Nutritional Labeling

The new health care law requires chain restaurants—defined as those with 20 or more locations—to provide calorie counts with standard menu items. Restaurants must also make available, upon request, additional nutritional information like the amount of total fat, saturated fat, cholesterol, sugar, and protein.

Vending machines run by chains—defined as an operator of 20 or more machines—also must prominently post nutrition labels for food and beverage selections.

The Food and Drug Administration (FDA) on April 1, 2011, released proposed rules on the labels. While drawing up the regulations, the FDA heard objections from theater chains that didn't want to put nutritional labels on popcorn loaded with fat calories. Theater owners said their primary business was providing entertainment, not selling food. So the proposed regulations exempt theaters, but did include concession stands and convenience stores.

The FDA at first expected to release final rules by the end of 2011, but the rules had not been released by August 2012. The agency had received mixed comments about requiring labels on vending machines. Some said the labels would be of little use since consumers are already familiar with the calorie content of products sold in vending machines. Others said vending machine labels would be useful because grouping items into categories, such as beverages, chips, and gums, allows easy comparisons. The proposed rules require vending machine labels to display a calorie count for each item sold.

In July 2012, US Representative John Carter (R-TX), introduced legislation that appeared to be an attempt to influence the rulemaking process. The legislation would exempt establishments that sell food not for immediate consumption. The Common Sense Nutrition Disclosure Act of 2012 also addressed the type of information that could appear on nutritional labels.

The Affordable Care Act's labeling law was supported by groups such as the American Heart Association, and was added to health care reform largely because of high levels of obesity and accompanying health problems. Table 9-1 shows US obesity rates for adults by state. For an adult, obesity is determined by weight and height.

Table 9-1. 2009 State Obesity Rates by Percentage of Adult Population

Arkansas: 30.5%	Maryland: 26.2%	Oregon: 23.0%
California: 24.8%	Massachusetts: 21.4%	Pennsylvania: 27.4%
Colorado: 18.6%	Michigan: 29.6%	Rhode Island: 24.6%
Connecticut: 20.6%	Minnesota: 24.6%	South Carolina: 29.4%
Delaware: 27.0%	Mississippi: 34.4%	South Dakota: 29.6%
District of Columbia: 19.7%	Missouri: 30.0%	Tennessee: 32.3%

Florida: 25.2%	Montana: 23.2%	Texas: 28.7%
Georgia: 27.2%	Nebraska: 27.2%	Utah: 23.5%
Hawaii: 22.3%	Nevada: 25.8%	Vermont: 22.8%
Idaho: 24.5%	New Hampshire: 25.7%	Virginia: 25.0%
Illinois: 26.5%	New Jersey: 23.3%	Washington: 26.4%
Indiana: 29.5%	New Mexico: 25.1%	West Virginia: 31.1%
Iowa: 27.9%	New York: 24.2%	Wisconsin: 28.7%
Kansas: 28.1%	North Carolina: 29.3%	Wyoming: 24.6%

Source: Centers for Disease Control.

RESTAURANTS ASSOCIATION FAVORS LABELS

The new nutrition labeling law was supported by the National Restaurant Association, which for years had resisted such an idea. But a national labeling law became palatable to the association after cities, counties, and states started passing a mish-mash of labeling laws that were confusing to consumers and restaurant owners.

So the federal law preempts all other laws. The association says it protects restaurants against nuisance lawsuits because it provides a reasonable standard that recognizes variability of food preparation, and allows labels to be based upon information from nutrient databases, cookbooks, and laboratory analyses.

Surprisingly, studies have shown that nutrition labels don't necessarily cause people to choose foods that are more healthful in fast-food restaurants. A far more influential factor is the placement of food selections on a menu. Studies show that in a fast-food setting, customers tend to ignore nutritional labels and order selections that are prominently displayed.

But nutrition and labels do influence restaurants and food manufacturers, often through media pressure. For example, when the government required trans fat labeling in 2003, many manufacturers and restaurants reformulated products because of media attention.

Moreover, nutritional labels are used by some customers, although there may not be enough of them to make a statistically significant blip in studies. For example, when New York City and Seattle passed nutritional labeling laws, restaurants reported that many customers were pleased to have the additional information.

Coming Next

There are a myriad of taxes included in health care reform. Most prominently, they include revenue-raising measures affecting the pharmaceutical industry, medical device manufacturers, and insurance companies. There is also a provision to increase the Medicare payroll tax. There's even a tax on tanning salons to help pay the cost of health care reform. In the next chapter, we'll look at some of the tax, revenue, and saving provisions that are included in the Affordable Care Act.

Who Pays?

Health Care Reform to Cost $1.1 Trillion

Ask many Americans about health care reform, even if they lack detailed knowledge of the new law, and they will express concern about whether the nation can afford it, according to polls. In other words, they may not know what it does, but they know it's going to cost plenty.

And they are right. Health care reform runs up big costs, mainly from expanding the Medicaid program, subsidizing private insurance for people with low incomes, and providing tax credits to small businesses.

The Congressional Budget Office in 2012 released an updated estimate indicating that health care reform will cost the US Treasury $1.1 trillion from 2012 to 2021. That's a big number, $1,100,000,000,000. The costs are primarily associated with covering the expansion of Medicaid and providing insurance subsidies to people with lower incomes.

The big question: who pays? The short answer is that we all do, but the longer answer is that much of the cost will be paid by insurers, pharmaceutical manufacturers, medical device makers, and taxpayers. Savings are supposed to be extracted from health care providers, mainly those associated with the Medicare program.

In this chapter, we'll look at provisions in the new health care law that raise revenues and save money. Some seem sound, but the effectiveness of others is doubtful.

■ **Note** The Congressional Budget Office's March 2012 estimate for the cost of health care reform, $1.1 trillion, is lower than its March 2011 estimate of $1.4 trillion. The cost is based upon a ten-year period, 2012–2021, and it keeps changing every year as legislative, economic, and technical aspects of health care reform change. For example, the Congressional Budget Office used an economic outlook for the 2012 estimate that reflected slower economic growth. The

March 2012 estimate also included updated projections for the rising cost of private health insurance premiums. Meanwhile, there were reductions in projected costs for tax credits for small businesses and subsidies for insurance exchanges.

HEALTH CARE SPENDING KEEPS RISING ON ALL FRONTS

Health care reform may lower government deficits, but health care costs still constitute a quickly growing portion of private and government spending. Consider the following trends:

- Health care costs represented 23 percent of the US budget spending in 2010, mostly for Medicare and Medicaid, and that is projected to rise to 29 percent by 2020.

- As a portion of the gross domestic product, which is a measure of all goods and services produced in the United States, federal health spending is expected to increase from 5.5 percent in 2010 to 7 percent by 2020.

- Total health spending, both government and private, is projected to increase from $2.6 trillion in 2010 to $4.6 trillion in 2019.

Medicare Tax Increase to Raise $210 Billion

One of the largest sources of revenue for health care reform is an increase in the Medicare Hospital Insurance tax—the "Medicare" tax taken out of each paycheck—for earned and unearned income over certain thresholds. This tax increase is expected to raise $210 billion between 2013 and 2019.

Beginning in 2013, the new law raises the Medicare Hospital Insurance tax by 0.9 percent for individuals with earned income of more than $200,000, and more than $250,000 for joint filers. For a couple filing separately, the threshold starts at $125,000 for each. Roughly, 1 in 50 US households have annual incomes greater than $250,000.

The existing Medicare Hospital Insurance tax is 1.45 percent for employees and 1.45 percent for employers. The employers' portion of the tax stays the same under the new health care law. For self-employed workers, the existing tax is 2.9 percent, and the 0.9 percent increase will be tacked onto income that exceeds thresholds.

There's a hazard for couples who together earn $250,000 or more, but neither of which earns more than $200,000. In those cases, employers will not have a trigger to increase withholding for the tax, and if employees don't adjust the withholding themselves, the government could require quarterly payments.

A March 23, 2010, report, "Tax Provisions in the Patient Protection and Affordable Care Act," by financial services giant Deloitte LLP, noted that a single taxpayer earning $500,000 will see a tax increase of about $2,700. A married couple filing jointly with the same income will see about a $2,250 increase.

In addition, the new health care law for the first time levies the entire 3.8 percent Medicare tax against unearned income that exceeds thresholds. Unearned income includes interest, dividends, capital gains, annuities, royalties, and rents. The tax will be applied to the lesser of taxpayer's net investment income or modified adjusted gross income that is in excess of the same dollar thresholds that apply to earned income.

Calculating this tax increase can get a little complicated. But as an example, the Deloitte analysis says a single taxpayer earning $1 million in wages and $100,000 in capital gains would owe an additional $11,000 in Medicare taxes under the new law—for earnings and capital gains. A married couple with the same earnings would pay an additional $10,550. Without the tax on the capital gains, the single taxpayer would see a $7,200 Medicare tax increase, and the couple would see a $6,750 increase.

"Cadillac" Insurance Tax Starts to Gear Up in 2018

The new health care law levies a 40 percent excise tax on high-end, private insurance policies, or so-called "Cadillac" plans, starting in 2018. The tax is paid by insurers and is expected to raise $12 billion its first year, $19 billion in 2019, and keep escalating thereafter.

The tax threshold is $10,200 for an individual policy and $27,200 for a family policy. The tax amounts to 40 percent of the policy's value above thresholds. For retirees and workers in high-risk jobs such as firefighting, the thresholds are set higher—$11,850 for an individual policy and $30,950 for a family policy.

Since the tax is being levied against insurers, it will likely be passed on to consumers in the form of higher premiums. Also, insurers or employers may increase deductibles or make other changes to policies to bring premium costs below thresholds and avoid the tax.

There is some confusion surrounding this tax because it was scheduled in the Senate-passed health care reform bill to go into effect in 2013. However, the Congressional Budget Office predicted that in 2016, nearly 20 percent of workplace policies would have been subject to this tax, and the measure was scaled back in final legislation.

Private Insurers to Pay Billions Annually in New Fees

Health care reform imposes billions of dollars in new annual fees on health insurance companies. The government expects these fees to raise $60 billion this decade.

The fees will be calculated by the US Treasury on the basis of each insurance company's share of the US market the previous year, as determined by net premiums written.

Fees begin at $8 billion a year in 2014 and increase to $14.3 billion in 2018. After that, they are indexed to the rate of premium growth. Table 10-1 shows a list of the nation's largest health insurance carriers and their revenue.

Table 10-1. The Top 10 US Insurance Companies by 2009 Total Revenue

Rank	Company	Revenue (in billions)
1	United Healthcare	$87.1
2	Wellpoint Group	$60.8
3	Kaiser Foundation Group	$42.1
4	Humana Group	$30.9
5	Aetna Group	$29.5
6	BC/BS of Michigan	$21.6
7	Cigna	$18.4
8	HCSC Group	$17.6
9	Coventry Health Care	$13.9
10	Highmark Group	$13.7

Source: For publicly traded companies, 10-K annual reports to the US Securities and Exchange Commission. For others, 2009 annual reports or press releases.

Drug Companies Start Paying New Fees in 2011

Pharmaceutical companies that manufacture, sell, or import drugs into the United States also must pay new fees under health care reform.

The fees are based upon the level of sales and market share. The fees started at $2.5 billion in 2011, and will rise to $4.1 billion in 2018. Then, fees drop to $2.8 billion for 2019 and thereafter. They are expected to raise $27 billion this decade. Table 10-2 shows the top ten pharmaceutical companies, ranked by US sales.

Table 10-2. Top 10 Drug Companies by US Sales

Rank	Company	2009 sales (in billions)
1	Pfizer	$27.8
2	Merck & Co.	$19.8
3	AstraZeneca	$19.8
4	GlaxoSmithKline	$15.0
5	Roche	$14.3
6	Novartis	$13.4
7	Eli Lilly & Co.	$13.2
8	Johnson & Johnson	$12.8
9	Amgen Corp.	$12.5
10	Teva USA	$12.1

Source: IMS Health and Charles Ornstein/ProPublica.

New Tax for Medical Devices Begins in 2013

The new health care law imposes a 3.2 percent excise tax on the sale of human medical devices. The tax must be paid by the manufacturer, producer, or importer of these devices.

The law excludes eyeglasses, contact lenses, hearings aids, and other devices that are generally purchased at retail stores for individual use. Home medical equipment such as wheelchairs and hospital beds are exempted, but there is uncertainty about whether respiratory health items such as oxygen machines will be exempted. The law also excludes medical devices for use in vessels or aircraft, and sales to state or local governments, nonprofit educational organizations, and qualified blood collection organizations.

The tax begins January 1, 2013, and is expected to raise $20 billion over ten years.

On June 7, 2012, the US House of Representative voted 270 to 146 to repeal the tax, but Senate leaders said they would block a vote on the measure. And even if it did clear the Senate, it would likely be vetoed by the president.

Critics of the tax say it will hurt companies that produce medical devices like MRI machines and pacemakers. Supporters of the tax say it is fair because health care reform will increase sales and use of medical devices.

Medicare Savings Estimate of Doubtful Accuracy

There is much doubt about health care reform's plan to save about $575 billion in the Medicare program over the first ten years. If accomplished, that kind of savings would significantly change the trajectory of Medicare spending, as shown in Figure 10-1.

Experts believe that about $300 billion of the savings are possible. Those initiatives include eliminating the Medicare Improvement Fund ($27 billion) in 2014, reducing payments to safety net hospitals ($50 billion), reducing Medicare Advantage plan payments ($145 billion), increasing the number of people paying Medicare Part B income-related premiums ($8 billion), and sticking to strict spending targets ($24 billion).

At issue, though, is about $233 billion in savings that are expected to come from permanently reducing payment updates for providers like nursing homes, hospitals, and home health agencies by about 1.1 percent a year from 2012 until 2021. Or, as Richard S. Foster, chief actuary for the Centers for Medicare & Medicaid Services, told a congressional committee on January 26, 2011, "It is important to note that the estimated savings for one category of Medicare provisions may be unrealistic."

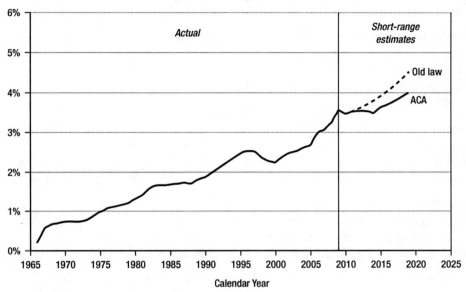

Medicare expenditures before and after the Affordable Care Act
(as a percentage of GDP)

Figure 10-1. The $575 billion in Medicare savings in the new health care law could lower the program's bite out of the gross domestic product by 0.5 percent. Source: Richard S. Foster, chief actuary, Centers for Medicare & Medicaid.

Foster agreed that the reductions would force providers to become more efficient by forming accountable care organizations (ACOs), using electronic medical records, and finding the most cost-efficient treatments.

But, he testified, providers must still deal with price increases for office space, utilities, and medical supplies. The result of cuts, he said, would be providers dropping out of the Medicare program and "possibly jeopardizing access to care for beneficiaries."

Most likely, Congress will monitor progress in this and intervene, thus significantly lowering the amount of savings now included in the Congressional Budget Office estimates.

Health Care Reform Puts a "Sin Tax" on Tanning Services

More and more, medical authorities are viewing indoor tanning as something akin to cigarette smoking—it is habitual, may cause cancer, and runs up medical costs. This emerging concern about tanning services set the stage for a tax to help offset the cost of health care reform while discouraging the use of tanning facilities.

America has a long history of creating these types of "sin taxes" to discourage behavior while making a little money for government operations. They are the type of taxes that stir up plenty of resentment, and health care reform's new tanning tax is no exception.

The new health care law includes a 10 percent tax on tanning services, which went into effect on July 1, 2010. The tax is expected to raise $2.7 billion over the next ten years. However, the Internal Revenue Service reported that receipts for the tax fell well behind estimates for fiscal year 2011. The IRS said some of the shortfall could be attributed to confusion about the new tax.

Tanning salon owners fumed when the new federal tax started, and complained bitterly that they had been targeted by the American Academy of Dermatology after the cosmetic industry had fought off government planners who wanted to institute a tax—a "Bo-Tax"—on some Botox procedures.

The Indoor Tanning Association is campaigning for repeal of the tax, and the group's president, Dan Humiston, says the tax has compounded job losses already suffered by the tanning industry because of the recession.

A TAN A DAY WON'T KEEP THE SKIN DOCTOR AWAY

Every day, about one million Americans step into tanning salons to darken their skin. These are mostly young white women. Whether they know it or not, they may be putting their lives at risk, according to many studies.

The American Academy of Dermatology reports that indoor tanning before the age of 35 increases the risk of developing the most deadly form of skin cancer, melanoma, by 75 percent.

Indoor tanning increases risks of deadly skin cancer, such as this melanoma.
Source: National Cancer Institute.

Exposure to UV radiation during indoor tanning damages DNA in cells. In addition to melanoma, it can lead to other skin cancers, premature skin aging, immune suppression, and eye damage, including cataracts and ocular melanoma.

The ultraviolet radiation used in tanning booths is classified by the International Agency for Research on Cancer as a Group 1 carcinogen, the same as tobacco smoke.

Recent studies have also shown that frequent tanners exhibit some of the same characteristics as substance abusers. Dermatologists have found that tanning makes the skin produce endorphins, and when researchers gave frequent tanners the anti-narcotic drug naltrexone, they developed symptoms consistent with addictive drug withdrawals. Other studies have found frequent tanners have higher anxiety levels and are more likely to use addictive substances.

The American Academy of Dermatology wants to do more than tax indoor tanning— it wants to ban it, particularly to minors.

Other Health Care Reform Revenue Sources

Health care reform has several smaller provisions to raise revenue to help pay for the Patient Protection and Affordable Care Act. Provisions that may affect individuals include:

- Limiting to $2,500 the contribution employees may make in accounts for so-called "cafeteria/flex" plans, starting in 2013. Previously, contributions had not been limited by law, and were often set at $5,000. This will reduce the amount of money people can set aside on a pre-tax basis, and raise an estimated $13 billion.

- Making over-the-counter drugs ineligible as a medical expense paid through any employer-provided coverage or any of the health savings account plans. This provision started January 1, 2011, and is expected to raise $1.4 billion.

- Raising the threshold for claiming an itemized deduction on income taxes from 7.5 percent to 10 percent of adjusted gross income. This starts in 2013, except for taxpayers or spouses who are over age 65. They may use the old threshold until 2017. This provision is expected to raise $15.2 billion.

- A fee on private health insurance plans, including self-insurance policies, to fund the Patient-Centered Outcomes

Research Institute. The fee starts at $1 in 2013 for each person covered, and increases to $2 in 2014. It is expected to raise $2.6 billion for the center. The fee will be paid by insurers, but the cost will likely be passed on to consumers.

Coming Next

Lawsuits have attempted to overturn it and politicians have tried to repeal it. Still, health care reform stands as the law of the land; but in the next chapter, we'll take a look at the future of health care reform and how it bodes, particularly in the 2012 presidential election.

War on Reform

New Law Faces Political Attacks

Since passage in 2010, health care reform has been under constant assault by lawsuits and Republican politicians on the state and federal levels. Proponents and opponents were locked in stalemate until June 28, 2012, when the US Supreme Court upheld key provisions of the Affordable Care Act, including the individual mandate. The legal ruling was a blow to opponents of health care reform, but opposition to the new law continued in the political arena.

On July 11, 2012, the US House of Representatives voted 244 to 185 to repeal health care reform. It was the thirty-third time that the Republican-led House attempted to kill the law; and like the previous attempts, it failed because the Senate and White House are controlled by Democrats.

Amid the legislative clatter, Mitt Romney, the Republican presidential candidate, vowed action to start repeal of the Affordable Care Act his first day in office, if elected. Meanwhile, states have passed a host of constitutional amendments, bills, provisions, and non-binding resolutions that attempt to block or modify different aspects of the Affordable Care Act.

We'll take a closer look at those developments in this final chapter and try to determine the alternatives if political challenges succeed in overturning all or a portion of the Patient Protection and Affordable Care Act of 2010.

Partisan Divide over Health Care Reform

The Supreme Court decision on the Affordable Care Act may have settled the issue of the individual mandate, but it left a partisan divide over health care reform. The new law has now evolved into a political litmus test. Democrats favor it and Republicans oppose it. Oddly, though, a Kaiser Health Tracking Poll taken immediately after the Supreme Court decision found that

46 percent of Americans still had fairly open minds about the health care reform—with 26 percent saying they had an opinion about the law, but it could change, and another 20 percent saying they had no opinion about it.

After the Supreme Court decision, Mitt Romney vowed to quickly repeal the Affordable Care Act. However, that seems more like a hasty promise made in the heat of a political debate than a realistic threat. For one thing, Romney himself has mixed feelings about the growing socialization of US medicine. While governor of Massachusetts, he championed a system of health care reform that provided the Obama Administration with a prototype for national reform. For years, Romney expressed pride in that accomplishment, but while running for president, he distanced himself from the experience because it ran contrary to conservative dogma. Nonetheless, Romney was still slipping off message, as he did during campaign trip to Israel when he gushed over that nation's ability to contain health care costs. He never mentioned that the Israel does this through a system of socialized medicine.

On a more practical level, for Romney to quickly repeal the Affordable Care Act, Republicans in the 2012 election would have to retain control of the House and gain 13 seats in the Senate to establish a 60-vote, filibuster-proof majority. Even the most optimistic of Republicans don't envision the GOP gaining that much power in the Senate.

Without a filibuster-proof Senate, Republicans would have to pass a spending measure in the House that would repeal health care reform. That would allow passage of a measure in the Senate by a simple majority. But mixing the repeal of health care reform with a national budget is a very complicated and tricky scenario, and one that would not evolve quickly, if at all.

In addition, it is doubtful that Republicans would really choose to repeal the entire Affordable Care Act anyway. Such an act would create chaos in the health care system, and it could easily lead to an economic catastrophe with severe political repercussions. For example, think about the confusion that would occur if the government suddenly eliminated the laws governing accountable care organizations, tougher fraud rules, and insurance regulations that have extended coverage to millions of Americans. That's not a pretty thought, even for Republican politicians.

But that does lead to the most likely and logical scenario if Romney is elected president—a piecemeal attack on the Affordable Care Act. Romney would be able to decide what provision of the Affordable Care Act to enforce and what provisions to ignore, and it would seem entirely possible for him to delay or even abolish something like the individual mandate, which is enforced through rules issued by the Internal Revenue Service.

At the very least, Romney would be in a powerful position that allowed him to pick and choose which provisions of health care reform to keep and which provisions to scrap.

Republicans Hope to Repeal and Replace Affordable Care Act

For years, Republicans have talked about repealing and replacing the Affordable Care Act. And they've floated out some proposals, although none have gained traction. The following are the general principles of Republican replacement plans:

- *Medical liability reform.* The GOP believes lawsuits have forced doctors to order costly and often unnecessary tests to protect themselves. This practice is often referred to as "defensive medicine." The GOP wants to rein in "junk lawsuits" to lower medical costs. A September 2010 study in *Health Affairs* by researchers from the Harvard School of Public Health, estimated the cost of defensive medicine to be about $55.6 billion a year, or 2.4 percent of annual health care spending.

- *Allow insurers to operate across state lines.* The GOP says Americans living in states with expensive health insurance plans need access to less expensive plans offered in other states. As it stands now, states regulate most insurance policies, and set rules for how much insurers must keep in reserve and the type of treatments that policies must cover. It is difficult for many insurers to meet regulations for all states. GOP lawmakers have repeatedly introduced the "Health Care Choice Act," which would allow consumers to buy health insurance across state lines.

- *Expand health savings accounts.* The GOP wants to improve this system so the tax-sheltering accounts can be used to fill coverage gaps in high-deductible insurance plans. Republicans also believe that over-the-counter drugs should be a qualified expense for these accounts. Health care reform places new limits on HSAs and similar accounts, and it has disqualified over-the-counter medications as an expense.

- *Cover patients with pre-existing conditions.* The GOP agrees that people with pre-existing conditions should be given the opportunity to purchase insurance. Republicans want to accomplish this through expansion of state high-risk pools and reinsurance programs. Republicans also want to make it illegal for insurance companies to use pre-existing conditions as a basis for denying coverage for someone who has had prior coverage. Like the new health care law, the GOP also wants to eliminate annual and lifetime spending caps on policies, and prevent insurers from rescinding, or dropping coverage when a policyholder gets sick.

- *Prohibit taxpayer funding of abortion.* The GOP wants a government-wide, permanent prohibition on taxpayer funding of abortion and subsidies for insurance coverage that includes abortion. They want a law that goes further than the existing Hyde Amendment, which is not a permanent law but a rider attached to appropriation bills to prevent federal spending for abortions except in cases of rape and incest or when a woman's life is endangered. Health care reform puts more of this power in the hands of individual states. Republicans also want laws allowing health care providers to opt out of participating in medical procedures that violate their consciences.

Republicans fielded a health care reform proposal in 2009 based on these principals. At that time, the Congressional Budget Office estimated the bill would have reduced the federal deficit by $68 billion over a decade and provided insurance for an additional 3 million Americans.

PAUL RYAN ELEVATES MEDICARE REFORM TO AN ELECTION ISSUE

Mitt Romney's selection of US Representative Paul Ryan (R-WI) as his candidate for vice president put a national spotlight on the issue of Medicare reform. Ryan has been involved with several attempts to transform Medicare into a plan that offers beneficiaries premium support vouchers to help purchase private insurance plans. Last year, he proposed a Medicare reform plan that he developed jointly with Senator Ron Wyden (D-OR).

Meanwhile, President Obama has remained staunchly supportive of a traditional Medicare benefits—without a voucher option. Studies have shown that transforming Medicare to premium support program would make it more costly for many seniors. Many of the president's visions for the future of Medicare are contained in the Affordable Care Act.

Romney also has a Medicare reform plan, which has many of the elements of the Ryan-Wyden plan. The following summarizes Medicare reform proposals being advanced by President Obama, Romney, and Ryan.

- President Obama would maintain traditional Medicare, but make payment reforms that encourage quality over quantity of services. He is focusing the program on eliminating fraud, waste, and abuse. The Office of Management and Budget estimates the president's "Budget for Fiscal Year 2013" would save Medicare and Medicaid $364 billion over the next decade. The president wants to eliminate the Sustainable Growth Rate formula and create a new physician payment system. He would generate savings in Medicare through an emphasis on wellness and better preventative care for chronic diseases. And he wants to empower the Independent Payment Advisory Board to lower costs.

- Romney wants to maintain traditional Medicare as an option, but allow beneficiaries to choose subsidies to purchase private insurance. He would increase the age of eligibility to keep pace with gains in longevity. Romney wants private insurers to competitively bid plans for Medicare beneficiaries. That bidding system would determine the level of support Medicare would provide to beneficiaries. For example, the "benchmark" for support might be set at the second lowest bid or the average of bids by private insurers. The theory is that competition will lower costs for health care.

- The Ryan-Wyden plan would open Medicare to private insurance plans in 2022. These plans would be required to offer the same essential benefits found in traditional Medicare, which would also continue to be available to beneficiaries. A Medicare exchange marketplace would supplant Medicare Advantage plans, and an annual competitive bidding process would determine the level of government support for beneficiaries. Either the second-least expensive plan or traditional Medicare would be used as a benchmark, depending on which one is least expensive. Growth of Medicare costs would be limited to growth of gross domestic product, plus 1 percent. Premium supports would be adjusted for income, or means tested. Also, in a recent interview, Wyden said that this plan would be unworkable without changes to Medicare included in the Affordable Care Act.

State Legislatures, Governors Oppose Affordable Care Act

Members of at least 45 state legislatures have proposed measures to limit, alter, or oppose the Patient Protection and Affordable Care Act of 2010, according to the National Conference on State Legislatures. At least 20 states have passed binding resolutions opposing broad elements of health care reform.

In addition, at least 27 states have proposed constitutional amendments, and 24 states have considered advisory or non-binding resolutions. Another 23 states have considered or have passed nullification or state sovereignty bills to prevent enforcement of Affordable Care Act provisions. These actions are expected to have little effect on health care reform since the Supreme Court has ruled that the law is constitutional.

Actions that states have taken against the Affordable Care Act as of July 2012 include the following:

- Five states—Missouri, Montana, New Hampshire, Utah, and Wyoming—passed restrictions on further compliance with the Affordable Care Act unless approved by the state legislature.

- Sixteen states had statutory or state constitutional language providing that state government would not implement mandates requiring the purchase of insurance by individuals or payments by employers. Since the Supreme Court upheld the mandate, it's doubtful any of these provisions will have any impact on the new law.

- Seven states—Georgia, Indiana, Missouri, Oklahoma, South Carolina, Utah, and Texas—had enacted laws to create Interstate Health Compacts to establish health programs operating outside the Affordable Care Act. These compacts will not block implementation of health care reform, however.

While publicly opposing the law, however, some state leaders also have been quietly seeking funding opportunities offered through health care reform.

After the Supreme Court ruling on June 28, 2012, several Republican governors announced that they would delay plans to develop health insurance exchanges until after the November 2012 presidential election.

Several states have also returned grants associated with the Affordable Care Act. They include:

- Kansas, which returned a $31 million Early Innovator Grant.

- Florida, which returned the $1 million awarded to begin planning for an exchange, and another $1 million that would have funded a system to monitor insurance rate changes.

- New Hampshire, which blocked a $610,000 federal planning contract to create a health insurance exchange.

- Wisconsin, which is expected to return a $37.6 million Early Innovator Grant.

Conclusion: Health Care Reform Takes Nation to Tipping Point

Like it or not, the US government is deeply involved in the American health care system, and its involvement is growing. Nearly 100 million Americans depend upon Medicare or Medicaid. About 8.3 million veterans depend upon the US Department of Veterans Affairs for health care, and about the same number of military personnel, retirees, and dependents depend upon Tricare, which is operated by the US Department of Defense Military Health System. The Federal Employees Health Benefit Program covers another 8 million federal workers, their families, and retirees. That's roughly 125 million Americans who fall under some sort of federal health plan.

Now consider that there are 50 million Americans without insurance in a total population of 310 million. That leaves about 135 million Americans with coverage under private insurance plans.

The Affordable Care Act adds about 16 million Americans to Medicaid, and another 16 million to private insurance, with government tax supports and subsidies. If you're still counting, the final total for government supported health coverage will exceed 167 million Americans in the next decade.

Clearly, we are very close to a tipping point in American health care where the public insurance sector outweighs the private insurance sector.

But it's not that simple. The public and private insurance sectors are melded together by shared payment methods, diagnostic codes, hospitals, doctors, and a host of other complex elements that make up the American medical care system.

This hybrid system is very expensive and complicated. The United States dedicates about 18 percent of its economy to medicine. Most developed nations have socialized systems that account for only about 10 percent of their economies.

Our public-private system has produced some extraordinary medical achievements. Among other things, the US medical system provides the best cancer care in the world. Medical centers like the Mayo Clinic and MD Anderson Cancer Center are legendary in providing the highest quality medical care available.

But the greatest criticism of American medicine lies in its inability to provide a reasonably high quality of health care to all Americans. In other words, American health care has come up short.

So now the question is: What do we do about it?

The Affordable Care Act attempts to answer that question. It would extend the reach of American health care, while cutting costs and increasing quality. It's difficult to say whether the new law will take us forward or backward. It will take decades to determine that. But it has launched us on a journey filled with twists and turns.

Bibliography

Introduction

Anderson, Chris. "HHS Renews Push to Enroll People in Pre-Existing Condition Insurance Plan." Healthcare Finance News, February 11, 2011. www.healthcarefinancenews.com/news/hhs-renews-push-enroll-people-pre-existing-condition-insurance-plan.

CBS News/New York Times Poll. "The Debate Over Health Care Reform." CBSNEWS.com, July 29, 2009. www.cbsnews.com/stories/2009/07/29/politics/main5196340.shtml.

Masiye, Felix et al. Removal of User Fees at Primary Health Care Facilities in Zambia. Luska, Zambia: University of Zambia, Department of Economics, 2008.

Parks, Dave. "Dying to Live: Following Transplant, Every Day is a Miracle." Birmingham (AL) News, November 16, 2004.

———. "Into the Heart of the AIDS War Zone: Critical State for a Rural Hospital." Birmingham (AL) News, March 15, 2005.

Statistical Abstract of the United States. National Health Expenditures. Washington, DC: US Census Bureau, 2011.

TransplantLiving.org. "Financing a Transplant." United Network for Organ Sharing. Accessed 2011. www.transplantliving.org/beforethetransplant/finance/costs.aspx.

Chapter 1

BarackObama.com. "Barack Obama and Joe Biden's Plan to Lower Health Care Costs and Ensure Affordable, Accessible Health Coverage for All." 2010.

BCBS.com. "History of Blue Cross Blue Shield." BlueCross BlueShield Association. www.bcbs.com/about/history/.

Corning, Peter A. "The Evolution of Medicare." Social Security Administration, 1969.

KFF.org. "Glossary of Key Health Reform Terms." Henry J. Kaiser Family Foundation. 2008. www.kff.org/healthreform/upload/7909.pdf.

————. "Summary of New Health Care Reform Law." Henry J. Kaiser Family Foundation, April 19, 2011. www.kff.org/healthreform/8061.cfm.

————. "The Uninsured: A Primer." Henry J. Kaiser Family Foundation, October 13, 2011. www.kff.org/uninsured/7451.cfm.

Meyer, Bill. "National Health Care Debate Goes Back to Theodore Roosevelt Plan in 1912." Cleveland Plain Dealer, August 12, 2009. www.cleveland.com/nation/index.ssf/2009/08/national_health_care_debate_ha.html.

Montopoli, Brian. "White House Releases Letter From Cancer Patient Natoma Canfield." CBSNews.com, March 4, 2010. www.cbsnews.com/8301-503544_162-6267519-503544.html.

OpenCongress.org. "H.R. 3590 – Patient Protection and Affordable Care Act, Official Summary." Sunlight Foundation. Accessed 2010. www.opencongress.org/bill/111-h3590/show.

Reinhardt, Uwe E. "The Perennial Quest to Lower Health Care Spending." New York Times, September 24, 2010. http://economix.blogs.nytimes.com/2010/09/24/the-perennial-quest-to-lower-health-care-spending/.

RPC.Senate.gov. "H.R. 3590: The Quality, Affordable Health Care for All Americans Act." Senate Republican Policy Committee, 2009.

Supreme Court of the United States. "National Federation of Independent Business et al v. Sebelius, Secretary of Health and Human Services, et al." Argued March 26–28, 2012. Decided June 28, 2012.

VA.gov. "VA History in Brief." US Department of Veterans Affairs. Accessed 2012. www.va.gov/opa/publications/archives/docs/history_in_brief.pdf.

White House. Remarks of President Barack Obama on Health Insurance Reform. Washington, DC: Office of the Press Secretary, 2010.

Wolffe, Richard. Revival: The Struggle for Survival Inside the Obama White House. New York, NY: Crown, 2010.

Chapter 2

Armstrong, Drew. "McDonald's, 29 Other Firms Get Health Care Coverage Waivers." Bloomberg Business News, October 7, 2010.

Brudereck, Jason. "Understanding Health Care Reform Phase One." Reading Eagle (PA), September 23, 2010.

Center for Consumer Information & Insurance Oversight. "Covering People with Pre-Existing Conditions: Report on the Implementation and Operation of the Pre-Existing Condition Insurance Plan Program." Centers for Medicare & Medicaid Services, February 23, 2012.

Centers for Medicare & Medicaid Services. Closing the Prescription Drug Coverage Gap. Washington, DC: US Department of Health and Human Services, 2010.

Cutter, Stephanie. Voices of Health Care Reform: James's Story. Washington, DC: White House Office of the Press Secretary, 2011.

Goldstein, Amy. "Study: 129 Million Have Pre-Existing Conditions." Washington Post, January 18, 2011.

HealthCare.gov. "A New Day for American Consumers." US Department of Health and Human Services, September 23, 2010. www.healthcare.gov/news/factsheets/overview.html.

———. "New Medicare Benefits for 2011." US Department of Health and Human Services. January 21, 2011. www.healthcare.gov/news/factsheets/new_medicare_benefits.html.

———. "New Plan Options for Federally Administered Pre-Existing Condition Insurance Plan in 2011." US Department of Health and Human Services. November 5, 2010. www.healthcare.gov/news/factsheets/new_plan_options_2011.html.

———. "The 80/20 Rule: Providing Value and Rebates to Millions of Consumers." US Department of Health and Human Services, June 21, 2012. www.healthcare.gov/law/resources/reports/mlr-rebates06212012a.html.

Hoover, Kent. "Uncertainty Surrounds Health Care Repeal." Business Journal of Portland, January 28, 2011.

How, Sabrina et al. Scoring a Healthy Future: The Commonwealth Fund Scorecard on Child Health System Performance, 2011. New York, NY: The Commonwealth Fund, 2011.

KFF.org. "Expanding Medicaid to Low-Income Childless Adults under Health Reform: Key Lessons from State Experiences." Henry J. Kaiser Family Foundation, July 2010. www.kff.org/medicaid/upload/8087.pdf.

Kliff, Sarah and J. Lester Feder. "Child-Only Health Plans Endangered." Politico.com, January 27, 2011. www.politico.com/news/stories/0111/48299.html.

Lindquist, Rick. "What is Your Health Insurance Rebate?" Zane Benefits Online, July 24, 2012.

NCSL.org. "Covering Young Adults Through Their Parents' or Guardians' Health Policy." National Conference of State Legislatures, September 23, 2010. www.ncsl.org/default.aspx?tabid=14497.

O'Brien, James. "Health Discount Scams Targeting Those Seeking Low-Cost Insurance." WalletPop.com, March 7, 2011. www.walletpop.com/2011/03/07/health-discount-scams-targeting-those-seeking-low-cost-insurance/.

Perera, Isabela. State by State Numbers—Who is Vulnerable if the Affordable Care Act is Dismantled. East Lansing, MI: States News Service, 2011.

Roan, Shari. "Indoor Tanning May Be Addictive." Los Angeles Times, April 20, 2010.

RWJF.org. "Small Business Tax Credits." Robert Wood Johnson Foundation, January 14, 2011. www.rwjf.org/coverage/product.jsp?id=71700.

Saint Louis, Catherine. "You're Going to Pay for That Tan." New York Times, December 22, 2009.

Seltz, Rhonda. "Insurance Companies Shun Healthy Kids." Roanoke Times, December 20, 2010.

Suchetka, Diane. "Keeping Up With Health Care Reform." Cleveland Plain Dealer, February 7, 2011.

Vasely, Rebecca. "High Risk, High Demand: $5 Billion Pool Opening in Some States." Modern Healthcare, July 26, 2010.

———. "Ready to Jump In? States Advancing Plans for High-Risk Insurance Pools, But Not Everyone is Ready—or Willing—to Make the Dive." Modern Healthcare, May 31, 2010.

Yin, Sandra. Enrollees in High-Risk Insurance Pools Double to 10,000. Washington, DC: FierceMarkets Inc., 2011.

Chapter 3

Adamy, Janet. "McDonald's May Drop Health Plan." Wall Street Journal, September 30, 2010. http://online.wsj.com/article/SB1000142405274870343 1604575522413101063070.html.

BlueCross Blue Shield of Tennessee Inc. "What Is the Difference Between Premium Tax Credits and Cost-Sharing Subsidies?" Health Insurance Exchange Update, April 4, 2012.

Chaikind, Hinda, and Chris L. Peterson. Individual Mandate and Related Information Under PPACA. Washington, DC: Congressional Research Service, 2010.

Frist, Bill. "Why Both Parties Should Embrace ObamaCare's State Exchanges." The Week, July 18, 2012.

HealthCare.gov. "Affordable Care Act and Immunization." US Department of Health and Human Services. Last modified January 20, 2012. www.healthcare.gov/news/factsheets/affordable_care_act_immunization.html.

———. "Community Health Centers and the Affordable Care Act." US Department of Health and Human Services, August 6, 2010. www.healthcare.gov/news/factsheets/increasing_access_.html.

———. "Health Insurance Exchanges: State Planning and Establishment Grants." US Department of Health and Human Services, March 22, 2011. www.healthcare.gov/news/factsheets/esthealthinsurexch.html.

———. "Keeping the Health Plan You Have." US Department of Health and Human Services, June 14, 2010. www.healthcare.gov/news/factsheets/keeping_the_health_plan_you_have_grandfathered.html.

———. "Preventive Services Covered Under the Affordable Care Act." US Department of Health and Human Services, September 23, 2010. www.healthcare.gov/law/about/provisions/services/lists.html.

———. "Protecting Consumers and Putting Patients Back in Charge of Their Care." US Department of Health and Human Services, July 21, 2010. www.healthcare.gov/news/factsheets/2010/07/putting-patients-back-in-charge.html.

"Individual Mandate in Health Care Reform Law Still Widely Unpopular: Poll." Harris Interactive/HealthDay poll, March 1, 2011. www.harrisinteractive.com/NewsRoom/PressReleases/tabid/446/mid/1506/articleId/704/ctl/ReadCustom%20Default/Default.aspx.

KFF.org. "Access to Abortion Coverage and Health Reform." Henry J. Kaiser Family Foundation, November 2010. www.kff.org/healthreform/upload/8021. pdf.

———. "Health Reform Subsidy Calculator." Henry J. Kaiser Family Foundation. Accessed 2011. http://healthreform.kff.org/SubsidyCalculator. aspx.

Lischko, Amy M. et al. The Massachusetts Commonwealth Health Insurance Connector: Structure and Function. New York, NY: The Commonwealth Fund, 2009.

"New Report: Individual Health Insurance Market Failing Consumers." The Commonwealth Fund, July 2009. www.commonwealthfund.org/Content/ News/News-Releases/2009/Jul/New-Report-Individual-Health-Insurance-Market-Failing-Consumers.aspx.

Pear, Robert. "Long-Term Care Program Needs Changes." New York Times. February 21, 2011.

Serafini, Marilyn Werber. "Bill Frist to GOP Governors: Get Cracking On Exchanges." Kaiser Health News, July 18, 2012.

US Treasury Department. "Treasury Lays the Foundation to Deliver Tax Credits to Help Make Insurance Affordable for Middle-Class Americans." Press release, August 12, 2011.

Wisconsin.gov. "Wisconsin Health Insurance Exchange prototype." Accessed 2011. https://exchange.wisconsin.gov.

Chapter 4

HealthAffairs.org. "Health Policy Brief: Small Business Tax Credits." Robert Wood Johnson Foundation, January 14, 2011. www.healthaffairs.org/ healthpolicybriefs/brief_pdfs/healthpolicybrief_38.pdf.

HealthCare.gov. "The Affordable Care Act's Early Retiree Reinsurance Program." US Department of Health and Human Services, October 4, 2010. www.healthcare.gov/news/factsheets/early_retiree_reinsurance_program. html.

———. "Increasing Choice and Saving Money for Small Business." US Department of Health and Human Services, June 27, 2010. www.healthcare. gov/news/factsheets/increasing_choice_and_saving_money_for_small_ businesses.html.

IRS.gov. "Form W-2 Reporting of Employer Sponsored Health Coverage." Internal Revenue Service Newsroom, 2012.

————. "Small Business Health Care Tax Credit: Frequently Asked Questions." Internal Revenue Service. www.irs.gov/newsroom/article/0,,id=220839,00. html. Last modified January 30, 2012.

————. "Small Business Tax Credit for Small Employers." Internal Revenue Service. www.irs.gov/newsroom/article/0,,id=223666,00.html. Last modified May 23, 2012.

Leonard, Bill. Does the Health Reform Law Really Create an Employer Mandate? Alexandria, VA: Society for Human Resource Management, 2010.

O'Connor, James T. "Patient Protection and Affordable Care Act: Implications of Status as a Grandfathered Plan." Benefits Quarterly (2011), 12–7.

Poe, Stephanie. "Supreme Court's Decision Puts Pressure on Employers to Implement Health Law or Face Penalties." Mercer LLC, June 28, 2012.

"Small Employer Health Tax Credit: Factors Contributing to Low Use and Complexity." US Government Accountability Office, May 14, 2012.

"What Health Care Reform Means for Your Business," CNN.com. March 22, 2010. http://money.cnn.com/2010/03/22/smallbusiness/small_business_health_reform/.

White House. Fact Sheet: Small Business Health Care Tax Credit. Washington, DC: Office of the Press Secretary, 2010.

Chapter 5

AHIP.org. "AHIP Statement on Health Care Reform Legislation." America's Health Insurance Plans. http://www.ahip.org/Issues/Affordable-Care-Act/.

Appleby, Julie. "Final Medical Loss Ratio Rule Rebuffs Insurance Agents." Kaiser Health News, December 2, 2011.

CMS/Office of Legislation. Medicare "Accountable Care Organizations" Shared Savings Program—New Section 1899 of Title XVIII. Washington, DC: Centers for Medicare & Medicaid Services, 2011.

DeNoon, Daniel J. "No More Co-pay for Birth Control." WebMD Health News, August 1, 2012.

Devers, Kelly and Robert Berenson. Can Accountable Care Organizations Improve the Value of Health Care by Solving the Cost and Quality Quandaries? Washington, DC: The Urban Institute, 2009.

Girion, Lisa. "Blue Cross Praised Employees Who Dropped Sick Policyholders, Lawmaker Says." Los Angeles Times, June 17, 2009.

Inglehart, John K. "Assessing an ACO Prototype—Medicare's Physician Group Practice Demonstration." New England Journal of Medicine, December 22, 2010. doi: 10.1066/NEJMp1013896.

Jost, Timothy Stoltzfus. "Writing New Rules for Insurers—Progress on the Medical Loss Ratio." New England Journal of Medicine, October 27, 2010. doi: 10.1056/NEJMp1011717.

Kavilanz, Parija. "Health Care Coverage: Big Changes in 2012." CNN.com, March 10, 2011. http://money.cnn.com/2011/03/10/news/economy/health_insurance_changes_by_employers/index.htm.

Reinhardt, Uwe E. "How Much Money Do Insurance Companies Make? A Primer." New York Times, September 25, 2009. http://economix.blogs.nytimes.com/2009/09/25/how-much-money-do-insurance-companies-make-a-primer/.

———. "Is 'Community Rating' in Health Insurance Fair?" New York Times. January 1, 2010, http://economix.blogs.nytimes.com/2010/01/01/is-community-rating-in-health-insurance-fair/.

———. "On Health Care, the Devil's in the Details." New York Times. September 3, 2010, http://economix.blogs.nytimes.com/2010/09/03/on-health-care-the-devils-in-the-details/.

———. "What Portion of Premiums Should Insurers Pay Our in Benefits?" New York Times. October 2, 2009, http://economix.blogs.nytimes.com/2009/10/02/what-portion-of-premiums-should-insurers-pay-out-in-benefits/.

Sebelius, Kathleen. "Statement by US Department of Health and Human Service Secretary on Final Rule Requiring Most Health Insurance Plans to Cover Preventive Services for Women Including Recommended Contraceptive Services." HHS Press Office, January 20, 2012.

Stanton, M.W. "The High Concentration of US Health Care Expenditures." Agency for Healthcare Research and Quality, June 2006. www.ahrq.gov/research/ria19/expendria.htm.

Chapter 6

AAMC.org. "AAMC Releases New Physician Shortage Estimates Post-Reform." Association of American Medical Colleges, September 30, 2010. https://www.aamc.org/newsroom/newsreleases/2010/150570/100930.html.

AcademyHealth. "The Impact of the Affordable Care Act on the Safety Net." AcademyHealth's National Health Policy Conference, April 2012.

Andrews, Michelle. "Some Medicare Practices Move to Monthly Membership Fees for Patients." KaiserHealthNews.org, 2011. www.kaiserhealthnews.org/ features/insuring-your-health/michelle-andrews-on-subscribing-to-primary-care.aspx.

Axon, R. Neal and Mark V. Williams. "Hospital Readmission as an Accountability Measure." Journal of the American Medical Association, February 2, 2011, 504–505.

Berkowitz, Scott A. "Accountable Care Organizations at Academic Medical Centers." New England Journal of Medicine, February 2, 2011. doi: 10.1056/ NEJMp1100076.

Camden Coalition of Healthcare Providers. "Medicaid ACO Demonstration Projects." 2012.

Center for Policy Research. Innovations in Reducing Preventable Hospital Admissions, Readmissions, and Emergency Room Use. Washington, DC: America's Health Insurance Plans, 2010.

CMS.gov. "EHR Incentive Programs." Centers for Medicare & Medicaid Services. Last modified August 2, 2012. www.cms.gov/Regulations-and-Guidance/Legislation/EHRIncentivePrograms/index.html?redirect=/ ehrincentiveprograms/.

———." New Affordable Care Act Program to Improve Care, Control Medicare Costs Off to a Strong Start." CMS Office of Public Affairs, April 10, 2012.

Community Oncology Alliance. "Center for Medicare & Medicaid Innovation Awards $19 Million Grant to Develop Oncology Medical Home Model." PRNewswire, August 1, 2012.

Connors, Elenora E. and Lawrence O. Gostin. "Health Care Reform: A Historic Moment in US Policy." Journal of the American Medical Association, June 23, 2010, 2521–2522.

Fairman, Julia A., John W. Rowe, Susan Hassmiller, and Donna E. Shalala. "Broadening the Scope of Nursing Practice." New England Journal of Medicine, December 15, 2010. doi: 10.1056/NEJMp1012121.

Hall, Mark A. "Rethinking Safety-Net Access for the Uninsured." New England Journal of Medicine, December 10, 2010. doi: 10.1056/NEJMp1011502.

HealthCare.gov. "Creating Jobs and Increasing the Number of Primary Care Providers." US Department of Health and Human Services. June 16, 2010.

Bibliography

www.healthcare.gov/news/factsheets/creating_jobs_and_increasing_primary_care_providers.html.

"HHS announces 89 New Accountable Care Organizations." HomeCare Magazine, July 16, 2012.

Jha, Ashish K. "Meaningful Use of Electronic Health Records." Journal of the American Medical Association, October 20, 2010, 1709–1710.

Katz, Mitchell H. "Future of the Safety Net Under Health Reform." Journal of the American Medical Association, August 11, 2010, 679–680.

Kohn, Linda T. et al. To Err is Human: Building a Safer Health System. Washington, DC: National Academy Press, 2000.

Ku, Leighton, Karen Jones, Peter Shin, Brian Bruen, and Katherine Hayes. "The States' Next Challenge—Securing Primary Care for Expanded Medicaid Populations." New England Journal of Medicine, January 26, 2011. doi: 10.1056/NEJMp1011623.

Laraque, Danielle, and Calvin C.J. Sia. "Health Care Reform and the Opportunity to Implement a Family-Centered Medical Home for Children." Journal of the American Medical Association, June 16, 2010, 2407–2408.

Lowrey, Annie, and Robert Pear. "Doctor Shortage Expected to Worsen with Health Law." New York Times, July 28, 2012.

McDermott, Jim. "Harnessing Our Opportunity to Make Primary Care Sustainable." New England Journal of Medicine, January 19, 2011. doi: 10.1056/NEJMp1014256.

Muhlestein, David, Andrew Crowshaw, Tom Merrill, and Christian Pena. "Growth and Dispersion of Accountable Care Organizations: June 2012 Update." Leavitt Partners, June 2012.

Rau, Jordan. "Medicare to Penalize 2,211 Hospitals for Excess Readmissions." Kaiser Health News, August 13, 2012.

Richman, Barak D., and Kevin A Schulman. "A Cautious Path Forward on Accountable Care Organizations." Journal of the American Medical Association, February 9, 2011, 602–603.

Zemel, Elliot, and Fenton Nelson. "What Hospitals Are Doing to Prevent Medicare Readmission Penalties." Becker's Hospital Review, May 23, 2012.

Chapter 7

Adamopoulos, Helen. "Fears of Medicare Advantage Catastrophe Laid to Rest with ACA Decision." The Medicare NewsGroup, July 20, 2012.

Antos, Joseph R., Mark V. Pauly, Gail R. Wilensky. "Bending the Cost Curve Through Market-Based Incentives." New England Journal of Medicine, August 1, 2012.

Budetti, Peter. "Assessing Medicare and Medicaid Program Integrity." Testimony before House Committee on Oversight and Government Reform, June 7, 2012.

Calmes, Jackie. "Delicare Pivot as Republicans Blast Rivals on Medicare Cuts." New York Times, July 27, 2012.

Chattopadhyay, Arpita, and Andrew B. Bindman. "Linking a Comprehensive Payment Model to Comprehensive Care of Frail Elderly Patients." Journal of the American Medical Association, November 3, 2010, 1948–1949.

Elhauge, Einer. "Robert's Real Long Game?" Atlantic, July 20, 2012.

HealthCare.gov. "Medicare Beneficiary Savings and the Affordable Care Act." US Department of Health and Human Services, February 2012. www.healthcare.gov/center/reports/affordablecareact.html.

Hirth, Richard A. "Fact/Fiction: Medicare Only Covers Acute Care: It Does Not Cover Preventive Care." The Medicare NewsGroup, January 26, 2012.

Kennedy, Kelly. "Doughnut Hole Drug Savings Hit $687 Million in First Half." USA Today, July 25, 2012.

KFF.org "Summary of Key Changes to Medicare in 2010 Health Reform Law." Henry J. Kaiser Family Foundation, 2010. www.kff.org/healthreform/upload/7948-02.pdf.

Medicare Trustees. "2012 Annual Report of the Boards of Trustees of the Federal Hospital Insurance and Federal Supplemental Medical Insurance Trust Funds." Communication, April 23, 2012.

Parks, Dave. "At Odds Over Plummeting Claims: CMS vs. Cramton." HomeCare Magazine, February 2012.

Pizzi, Richard. "Florida Long-Term Care Providers Issue Warning on Medicaid, Medicare Cuts." HealthCare Finance News, May 13, 2010. www.healthcarefinancenews.com/news/florida-long-term-care-providers-issue-warning-medicaid-medicare-cuts.

Potetz, Lisa. "Medicare Spending and Financing: A Primer." Health Policy Alternatives Inc., February 2011.

Reinhardt, Uwe E. "How Medicare Pays Physicians." New York Times, December 3, 2010. http://economix.blogs.nytimes.com/2010/12/03/how-medicare-pays-physicians/.

————. "The Annual Drama of the 'Doc Fix.'" New York Times, December 17, 2010. http://economix.blogs.nytimes.com/2010/12/17/the-annual-drama-of-the-doc-fix/.

Sjoerdma, Donald. "Court's Decision on ACA Allows Medicare Economic Provisions to Unfold." The Medicare NewsGroup, June 28, 2012.

Smith, Donna. "Q+A: How Does Healthcare Overhaul Affect Medicare?" Reuters, March 22, 2010. www.reuters.com/article/2010/03/22/us-usa-healthcare-medicare-idUSTRE62JIFS20100322.

Chapter 8

Congressional Budget Office. "Estimates of the Insurance Coverage Provisions of the Affordable Care Act Updated for the Recent Supreme Court Decision." July 2012.

Cowen, Tyler. "The New Tug of War Over Medicaid." New York Times, July 14, 2012.

Galewitz, Phil. "Study: Nearly A Third of Doctors Won't See New Medcaid Patients." Kaiser Health News and Philadelphia Inquirer, August 6, 2012.

"GOP Governors Respond to CMS Signs of Flexibility Regarding Medicaid Expansion." Kaiser Health News, August 9, 2012.

Hancock, Jay. "Businesses Will Push Perry to Rethink Medicaid Expansion." Kaiser Health News, July 18, 2012.

Holahan, John, and Irene Headen. "Medicaid Coverage and Spending in Health Care Reform: National and State-by-State Results for Adults at or Below 133% FPL." Kaiser Commission on Medicaid and the Uninsured, May 2010.

KFF.org. "Medicaid and Children's Health Insurance Program Provisions in the New Health Reform Law." Henry J. Kaiser Family Foundation. April 7, 2010. www.kff.org/healthreform/7952.cfm.

————. "Medicaid Health Homes for Beneficiaries with Chronic Conditions." Kaiser Commission for Medicaid and the Uninsured, August 2012.

————. "Who Benefits from the ACA Medicaid Expansion." The Kaiser Commission on Medicaid and the Uninsured, 2012.

Kliff, Sarah. "The Cost of Medicaid Opt-Outs." Washington Post, July 24, 2012.

"Medicaid Official Outlines State Flexibility in Health Law's Medicaid Expansion." Kaiser Health News, August 7, 2012.

Sarafini, Marilyn Werber. "How the Scotus Medicaid Ruling Could Save Money." Kaiser Health News and Politico Pro, July 11, 2012.

Siegel, Bruce. "NAPH Deeply Concerned by Decisions to Reject Medicaid Expansion." National Association of Public Hospitals and Health Systems, July 12, 2012.

Sommers, Benjamin D. and Arnold M. Epstein. "Medicaid Expansion: The Soft Underbelly of Health Care Reform?" New England Journal of Medicine, November 24, 2010. doi: 10.1056/NEJMp1010866.

UnitedHealthcare. "Proposed Rule on Fee Increase for Medicaid Primary Care Physicians." May 11, 2012.

Chapter 9

AHRQ.gov. "Low Health Literacy Linked to Higher Risk of Death and More Emergency Room Visits and Hospitalizations." Agency for Healthcare Research and Quality, March 28, 2011. www.ahrq.gov/news/press/pr2011/lowhlitpr. htm.

Bompey, Nanci. "Bill Seeks to Limit Scope of ACA Menu Labeling Requirements Ahead of Rule." InsideHealthPolicy.com, July 25, 2012.

Boodman, Sandra G. "Helping Patients Understand Their Medical Treatment." Kaiser Health News, March 1, 2011. www.kaiserhealthnews.org/Stories/2011/ March/01/Health-Literacy-Understanding-Medical-Treatment.aspx.

CDC.gov. "US Obesity Trends by State 1985–2009." Centers for Disease Control. www.cdc.gov/obesity/data/trends.html. Last modified August 2012.

Drummond, Kate. "Hidden Health Care Clause: Menu Labels Go National." AolNews.com, March 22, 2010. www.aolnews.com/2010/03/22/hidden-health-care-clause-menu-labels-go-national/.

Health.gov. "National Action Plan to Improve Health Literacy." US Department of Health and Human Services, June 28, 2010. www.health.gov/communication/ HLActionPlan/.

HHS.gov. "HHS Releases National Plan to Improve Health Literacy." US Department of Health and Human Services, May 27, 2010. www.hhs.gov/ash/news/20100527.html.

————. "Medicare Payment and Volume Data." US Department of Health and Human Services. www.hospitalcompare.hhs.gov. Last modified July 19, 2012.

Medicare.gov. "Home Health Compare." US Department of Health and Human Services. www.medicare.gov/HomeHealthCompare/search.aspx. Last modified July 19, 2012.

Moore, Cynthia A. "PPACA Update: Summary of Benefits for a Group Helath Plan." Dickinson Wright PLLC, April 17, 2012.

Somers, Stephen A., and Roopa Mahadevan. Health Literacy Implications of the Affordable Care Act. Hampton, NJ: Center for Health Care Strategies Inc., 2010.

Vaida, Bara. "Calorie Labeling for Restaurant Recommendations Coming Soon." Kaiser Health News, March 6, 2011. www.kaiserhealthnews.org/Stories/2011/March/07/menu-labeling.aspx.

WCSR.com. "FDA Expediting Menu Labeling Implementation and Enforcement." Womble Carlyle Sandridge & Rice, PLLC. August 29, 2010. www.wcsr.com/client-alerts/fda-expediting-menu-labeling-implementation-and-enforcement.

Chapter 10

Deloitte.com. "Prescription for Change 'Filled.' Tax Provisions in the Patient Protection and Affordable Care Act." Deloitte Development LLC. Accessed 2010. www.deloitte.com/view/en_US/us/Services/tax/112a52f1b5277210Vgn VCM100000ba42f00aRCRD.htm.

"Dollars for Docs." National Public Radio, August 23, 2010. www.npr.org/series/130598927/dollars-for-docs-how-pharma-money-influences-physician-prescriptions.

Elmendorf, Douglas W. "Testimony on Last Year's Health Care Legislation." Congressional Budget Office. Accessed 2011. http://cboblog.cbo.gov/?p=2088.

Foster, Richard S. "The Estimated Effect of the Affordable Care Act on Medicare and Medicaid Outlays and Total National Health Care Expenditures. Testimony Before the House Committee on the Budget." US House of Representatives Committee on the Budget, January 26, 2011. http://budget.house.gov/UploadedFiles/fostertestimony1262011.pdf.

HealthCare.gov. "Centers for Medicare & Medicaid Services Enhance Efforts to Prevent and Fight Health Care Fraud." US Department of Health and Human Services, December 16, 2010. www.healthcare.gov/news/factsheets/prevent_health_care_fraud.html.

Holahan, John and L. Blumberg. "Will Health Care Reform Increase the Deficit and National Debt?" The Urban Institute, 2010. www.rwjf.org/healthpolicy/product.jsp?id=66768.

Kumar, Kavita. "Tanning Owners Do Slow Burn Over Tax." St. Louis Post-Dispatch, July 1, 2010.

Nevius, Alistair. "Health Care Reform Reshapes Tax Code." Journal of Accountancy, April 1, 2010.

Pryde, Joan. "Health Care Reform: 13 Tax Changes on the Way." Kiplinger, October 8, 2010. www.kiplinger.com/businessresource/forecast/archive/health-care-reform-tax-hikes-on-the-way.html?si=1.

Waller Lansden Dortch & Davis LLP. "Follow the Money: Healthcare Reform Revenue Raising (Tax) Provisions," March 23, 2010. www.wallerlaw.com/articles/2010/03/23/follow-the-money-the-healthcare-reform-revenue-raising-tax-provisions.

Chapter 11

Blumberg, Linda J. "How Will the PPACA Impact Individual and Small Group Premiums in the Short and Long Term?" The Urban Institute, July 2010. www.urban.org/uploadedpdf/412128-PPACA-impact.pdf.

CBO.gov. "Effects of Eliminating the Individual Mandate to Obtain Health Insurance." Congressional Budget Office, March 2010. www.cbo.gov/ftpdocs/113xx/doc11379/Eliminate_Individual_Mandate_06_16.pdf.

Fleming, Matthew, and David Schultz. "Mitt Romney on Health Care." Kaiser Health News, August 1, 2012.

Goldstein, Amy, and N.C. Aizenman. "As Health Care Law Turns 1, Supporters Using Occasion to Shape It's Image." Washington Post, March 22, 2011.

GOP.gov. "Repeal & Replace the Job Destroying Health Care Law." The House Republican Conference, January 2011. www.gop.gov/pledge/healthcare.

HealthCare.gov. "The Price of Repealing the Affordable Care Act." US Department of Health and Human Services, January 7, 2011. www.healthcare.gov/news/factsheets/repealcosts.html.

Herring, Bradley. "An Economic Perspective on the Individual Mandate's Severability from the ACA." New England Journal of Medicine, February 23, 2011. doi: 10.1056/NEJMpv1101519.

Hsiao, William C. "State-Based Single-Payer Health Care—A Solution for the United States?" New England Journal of Medicine, March 16 2011. doi: 10.1056/NEJMp1100972.

JLBGHealth.com. "Judge Says NH Man Lacks Standing to Sue Over Health Care Reform." J.L. Barnes Group, April 4, 2011. www.jlbghealth.com/blog/archives/963-Judge-says-NH-man-lacks-standing-to-sue-over-healthcare-reform.html.

Kenen, Joanne. "Experts Ponder 'Plan B' Options for the Individual Mandate." Henry J. Kaiser Family Foundation, December 17, 2010. www.kaiserhealthnews.org/Stories/2010/December/17/mandate-alternatives.aspx.

Kennedy, Kelly. "States Proceed on Health Care Law." USA Today, February 18, 2011.

KFF.org. "A Guide to the Supreme Court's Affordable Care Act Decision." Henry J. Kaiser Family Foundation, July 2012.

————. "Health Tracking Poll: Exploring the Public's View on the Affordable Care Act." Henry J. Kaiser Family Foundation, July 2012.

————. "Pop Quiz: Assessing Americans' Familiarity with the Health Care Law." Henry J. Kaiser Family Foundation. February 2011. www.kff.org/healthreform/upload/8148.pdf.

Kliff, Sarah. "Romney Praises Health Care in Israel, Where Strong Government Influence Has Driven Down Costs." Washington Post, July 30, 2012.

Lizza, Ryan. "Why Romney Won't Repeal Obamacare." New Yorker, June 28, 2012.

Medicare NewsGroup. "Romney Picks Ryan as Vice-Presidential Running Mate, Heats up Medicare Debate." Media Coverage Roundup, August 2012.

————. "What Is President Obama's Position on Medicare Reform?" FAQ, 2012.

————. "What Are Republican Presidential Candidate Mitt Romney's Views on Medicare Reform?" FAQ, 2012.

NCLS.org. "State Legislation and Actions Challenging Certain Health Reforms, 2011–2012." National Conference of State Legislatures. www.ncsl.org/issues-research/health/state-laws-and-actions-challenging-aca.aspx. Last modified August 10, 2012.

Oberlander, Jonathan. "Beyond Repeal—The Future of Health Care Reform." New England Journal of Medicine, November 17, 2010. doi: 10.1056/ NEJMp1012779.

————. "Under Siege—The Individual Mandate for Health Insurance and Its Alternatives." New England Journal of Medicine, February 16, 2011. doi: 10.1056/NEJMp1101240)

Rutkow, Lainie, and Stephen P. Teret. "Role of State Attorneys General in Health Policy." Journal of the American Medical Association, September 22, 2010, 1377–1378.

Sarafini, Marilyn Werber. "How Paul Ryan Proposes to Change Medicare." Kaiser Health News, August 11, 2012.

Taylor, Andrew. "Repealing Obama's Health Care Law Won't Be Easy." Associated Press, June 28, 2012.

TheHill.com. "Number of Healthcare Reform Law Waivers Climbs to Above 1,000." The Hill, March 6, 2011. http://thehill.com/blogs/healthwatch/health-reform-implementation/147715-number-of-healthcare-reform-law-waivers-climbs-above-1000.

Vermont.gov. "Vermont Blueprint for Health." State of Vermont, January 26, 2011. http://hcr.vermont.gov/sites/hcr/files/final_annual_report_01_26_11.pdf.

Zelizer, Julian E. "The Real Threat to Health Care Reform." CNN.com, December 20, 2010. http://articles.cnn.com/2010-12-20/opinion/zelizer.health.reform.threat_1_health-care-republicans-policies?_s=PM:OPINION.

I

Index

CPSIA information can be obtained at www.ICGtesting.com
Printed in the USA
LVOW122017301012

305104LV00001B/1/P